Excellent English 2
Language Skills for Success

Jan Forstrom
Mari Vargo

Marta Pitt
Shirley Velasco

Mc
Graw
Hill

Excellent English Student Book 2

ISBN 13: 978-0-07-719764-3 (Student Book)
ISBN 10: 0-07-719764-X
2 3 4 5 6 7 8 9 10 QVS 18 17 16 15 14

ISBN 13: 978-0-07-719772-8 (Student Book REPRISION)
ISBN 10: 0-07-719772-0
2 3 4 5 6 7 8 9 10 QVS 18 17 16 15 14

Series editor: Nancy Jordan
Developmental editors: Nancy Jordan, Jenny Bixby
Cover designer: Witz End Design
Interior designer: NETS
Compositor: NETS

The credits section for this book begins on page 222 is considered an extension of the copyright page.

The **McGraw·Hill** Companies

Acknowledgements

The authors and publisher would like to thank the following individuals who reviewed the *Excellent English* program at various stages of development and whose comments, reviews, and field-testing were instrumental in helping us shape the series.

Tony Albert • Jewish Vocational Service; San Francisco, CA

Robert Breitbard • Collier County Adult Education; Naples, FL

Jeff Bright • McHenry County College; Crystal Lake, IL

Sherrie Carroll • Montgomery College; Conroe, TX

Georges Colin • Lindsey Hopkins Technical Education Center; Miami, FL

Irene Dennis • Palo Alto College; Palo Alto, CA

Terry Doyle • City College of San Francisco, Alemany Campus; San Francisco, CA

Rolly Fanton • San Diego City College; San Diego, CA

Colleen Fitzmaurice • San Diego Community College District, Mid-City; San Diego, CA

Phil Garfinkel • Adult & Family Education of Lutheran Medical Centers; Brooklyn, New York

Ana Maria Guaolayol • Miami-Dade College, Kendall Campus; Miami, FL

Margaret Hass • San Diego Community College District, Mid-City; San Diego, CA

Giang Hoang • Evans Community Adult School, Los Angeles Unified School District; Los Angeles, CA

Armenuhi Hovhannes • City College of San Francisco, Mission Campus; San Francisco, CA

Vivian Ikeda • City College of San Francisco, Teacher Resource Center; San Francisco, CA

Sally Ruth Jacobson • San Diego Community College District, Centre City; San Diego, CA

Kathleen Jimenez • Miami-Dade College Kendall Campus; Miami, FL

Nancy Johansen • San Diego Community College District, Mid-City; San Diego, CA

Mary Kapp • City College of San Francisco, Chinatown Campus; San Francisco, CA

Caryn Kovacs • Brookline Adult Education; Brookline, MA

Linda Kozin • San Diego Community College District, North City Center; San Diego, CA

Gretchen Lammers-Ghereben • Martinez Adult Education School; Martinez, CA

Paul Mayer • Glendale Community College; Glendale, CA

Lee Mosteller • San Diego Community College District, North City; San Diego, CA

Iliana Pena • Lindsey Hopkins Technical Education Center; Miami, FL

Howard Riddles • Tomlinson Adult Learning Center; St. Petersburg, FL

Lisa Roberson • Mission Language and Vocational School; San Francisco, CA

Renata Russo Watson • Harris County Department of Education; Harris County, TX

Francisco Sanchez • Miami-Dade College, Kendall Campus; Miami, FL

Curt Sanford • City College of San Francisco, Alemany Campus; San Francisco, CA

Laurie Shapero • Miami-Dade College, Kendall Campus; Miami, FL

Eileen Spada • Max Hayes Adult School; Detroit, IL

Margaret Teske • Mt. San Antonio College; Walnut, CA

Theresa Warren • East Side Independence Adult Center; San Jose, CA

D. Banu Yaylali • Miami-Dade College, Kendall Campus; Miami, FL

Scope and Sequence

Unit	Grammar	Vocabulary	Listening/ Speaking/ Pronunciation	Reading	Writing
Pre-Unit *page 2*	• Nouns • Pronouns • Adjectives • *Be* • Punctuation	• Alphabet • Greetings • Months	• Spell names and places aloud • Ask for personal information • Introduce a classmate • **Pronunciation:** say dates	• Read a story about a classmate.	• Write descriptive sentences
1 **Family and Education** *page 6*	• Simple present of *be*: Statements and contractions. • Contrast *be* and *have* • Simple present of *be*: *Yes/No* and information questions	• Family relationships • Descriptive adjectives • Physical characteristics • Types of schools in U.S. • Grade levels	• Identify relationships • Talk about physical characteristics • Report a lost person • Register for school • Talking about education • **Pronunciation:** Say ordinal and cardinal numbers	• Scan a school flyer for specific information • Read about levels of education and related income • Interpret a bar graph	• Use capital letters and periods to construct sentences • Combine sentences to form a paragraph • Write a paragraph describing yourself
2 **In the Community** *page 22*	• Present continuous: statements, spelling rules, *yes/no* questions, information questions • Polite requests and offers with *can, could, may* and *would*	• Places and activities in the community: library, bank, post office, mall • Shopping terms	• Conduct personal business in the community. • Communicate by telephone • Talk about activities happening now • Initiate and respond to requests • Make polite offers • **Pronunciation:** *Could you*	• Read and interpret rules and fee information • Scan an email for key information • Identify the main idea of an email	• Use the appropriate greeting in written and electronic correspondence • Edit an informal email for proper punctuation and capitalization • Write an informal email message
3 **Daily Activities** *page 38*	• Simple present: Statements, spelling rules • Adverbs of frequency • Expressions of frequency	• Daily activities: home and school • Classroom routines • Learning strategies	• Describe your personal schedules • Talk about classroom routines • Welcome a new student • Make appointments for personal business • **Pronunciation:** Final *s* sounds: *s, z,* and *iz*	• Read for time expressions to find the order of events • Predicting the content of a story from the title • Read a class schedule • Read personal stories	• Create titles for compositions • Write about daily routines • Make a personal schedule • Fill out a school registration form • Write about your typical day
4 **Finding a Job** *page 54*	• Simple present: *yes/no* questions • Simple present: Information questions	• Job positions and responsibilities • Job requirements • Job benefits • Want ad terms and abbreviations • Job application terms • Educational achievement • Pay stub information	• Ask and answer questions about work responsibilities, schedules, benefits and requirements for jobs • Express opinions about work • Inquire about a job opening • **Pronunciation:** Questions with *does he* or *does she*	• Scan a form to find specific information • Interpret basic abbreviations in job ads • Read and interpret a job application	• Properly fill out and check a form requiring personal information • Fill out a job application • Write lists identifying job requirements, responsibilities and benefits • Take notes on job information presented orally

Civics/Lifeskills	Math	Critical Thinking	Correlations		
			CASAS	SCANS	EFF Content Standards
• Spell names of people and places	• Say birthdates	• Name the letters of the alphabet	• 0.1.4, 0.1.6, 0.2.1, 2.3.2	• Interprets and communicates information • Participates as a member of a team	• Speak so others can understand • Listen actively
• Describe a lost child • Understand the U.S. educational system • Complete a school registration form	• Calculate ages • Ordinal and cardinal numbers	• Listen and understand public address announcements • Analyze information in a graph format	• **1:** 0.1.2, 0.2.1, 2.6.4 • **2:** 7.2.1, 0.1.6 • **3:** 0.2.1, 0.1.2 • **5:** 0.2.1 • **6:** 0.2.1, 0.1.2, 0.2.2 • **7:** 0.1.6	• Interprets and communicates information • Participates as a member of a team • Acquires and evaluates information • Organizes and maintains information	• Listen actively • Speak so others can understand • Convey ideas in writing • Read with understanding • Use math to solve problems and communicate
• Use community resources such as the library, bank, and post office	• Calculate late fees at the library	• Practice making requests at the library • Analyze sentences for errors • Review an email message • Compose a message to a friend about current activities	• **1:** 0.1.6 • **2:** 0.1.6 • **3:** 0.16 • **4:** 0.1.3, 0.1.2 • **5:** 0.1.3, 1.3.3, 1.6.3 • **6:** 2.6.4 • **7:** 0.1.2, 0.2.4	• Acquires and evaluates information • Organizes and maintains information • Participates as a member of a team • Negotiates	• Convey ideas in writing • Listen actively • Cooperate with others • Read with understanding • Use math to solve problems and communicate • Advocate and Influence
• Make appointments • Communicate schedule information at home, school and work	• Complete a bar graph showing survey results	• Identify and list daily activities • Analyze the ways you learn English	• **1:** 0.1.6 • **2:** 0.2.1, 0.1.2 • **3:** 2.3.2 • **4:** 7.2.1 • **5:** 2.6.1, 2.6.2, 2.3.2 • **6:** 0.1.2, 0.1.6, 0.2.1, 2.5.5, 2.6.1, 2.6.2, 7.4.1 • **7:** 0.1.2, 2.5.5 • **8:** 0.2.1, 0.1.2, 7.4.1	• Interprets and communicates information • Participates as a member of a team • Acquires and evaluates information • Allocates time • Allocates material and facility resources • Allocates human resources	• Listen actively • Speak so others can understand • Convey ideas in writing • Plan • Read with understanding • Use math to solve problems and communicate • Observe critically
• Use the services at the Department of Motor Vehicles • Practice having a job interview • Read newspaper job ads • Complete a job application	• Calculate net pay	• Assess what job benefits are important to you • Identify different types of diplomas and educational certificates • Analyze newspaper job ads • Review a completed form for accuracy	• **1:** 4.4.2, 4.61 • **2:** 0.2.1, 4.1.5, 4.1.6, 4.1.7 • **3:** 0.2.1, 0.1.2, 4.1.5, 4.1.6, 4.1.7 • **4:** 4.8.1, 4.8.2 • **5:** 0.2.2, 4.1.2, 4.2.1 • **6:** 4.1.3, 7.4.1 • **7:** 0.2.2, 4.1.2 • **8:** 4.1.5, 0.2.1, 4.1.6, 4.1.7	• Interprets and communicates information • Negotiates • Acquires and evaluates information • Serves clients/customers • Works with cultural diversity • Allocates human resources	• Speak so others can understand • Observe critically • Listen actively • Read with understanding • Plan • Cooperate with others • Convey ideas in writing • Use math to solve problems and communicate

Civics/Lifeskills	Math	Critical Thinking	Correlations		
			CASAS	SCANS	EFF Content Standards
• Visit the emergency room • Make a doctor's appointment • Read medicine labels • Practice making a 911 emergency call	• Calculate dosages	• Recognize and describe symptoms • Name illnesses • Distinguish good and bad health habits • Interpret warning labels	• **1:** 3.1.1, 3.1.2, 3.2.1 • **2:** 2.5.3, 3.1.3 • **3:** 3.1.1, 3.1.2 • **4:** 3.1.2, 3.2.1 • **5:** 3.2.1, 3.3.1, 3.3.3, 3.3.2 • **6:** 3.4.3 • **8:** 3.4.3, 4.3.4	• Acquires and evaluates information • Participates as a member of a team • Interprets and communicates information • Organizes and maintains information	• Speak so others can understand • Observe critically • Convey ideas in writing • Listen actively • Plan • Use math to solve problems and communicate • Read with understanding
• Read a work schedule • Prepare a work schedule • Report progress at work	• Calculate hours on a work schedule	• Understand scheduled versus actual time worked • Express the characteristics of an enjoyable job	• **1:** 7.4.5 • **2:** 4.6.1 • **3:** 7.4.8 • **4:** 0.2.2, 4.1.2 • **5:** 4.1.5, 0.2.1, 4.1.5, 4.1.6, 4.1.7 • **6:** 4.1.3, 4.4.1, 4.4.3, 4.6.5 • **7:** 4.1.5, 0.2.1, 4.1.5, 4.1.6, 4.1.7 • **8:** 0.2.1, 4.1.5, 4.1.6, 4.1.7	• Negotiates • Interprets and communicates information • Acquires and evaluates information • Organizes and maintains information	• Convey ideas in writing • Listen actively • Speak so others can understand • Observe critically • Convey ideas in writing • Read with understanding • Use math to solve problems and communicate
• Compare towns and neighborhoods • Relate your personal history	• Say large numbers	• Make historical comparisons • Relate emotions to a variety of situations	• **1:** 7.4.5 • **2:** 2.3.2, 2.3.3 • **3:** 7.2.1, 7.4.2 • **6:** 1.4.2, 0.1.2 • **7:** 7.2.1 • **8:** 7.2.1, 7.4.2	• Interprets and communicates information • Acquires and evaluates information • Allocates money • Organizes and maintains information	• Listen actively • Observe critically • Convey ideas in writing • Plan • Use math to solve problems and communicate • Read with understanding
• Practice ordering and taking an order in a restaurant • Describe good eating habits • Analyze a recipe	• Calculate prices	• Calculate a restaurant bill • Interpret nutrition labels • Compare the nutritional value of different foods • Evaluate your own eating habits	• **1:** 1.6.1, 7.4.5 • **2:** 1.2.1, 1.6.1, 3.5.1, 1.1.7, 1.3.8 • **3:** 0.1.4, 2.6.4, 1.1.7, 1.3.8 • **4:** 1.3.8, 1.6.1, 3.5.1, 3.5.2, 3.5.3, 7.4.5 • **5:** 1.2.1, 1.6.1, 3.5.1 • **6:** 1.2.1, 1.6.1, 3.5.1 • **7:** 7.2.1, 7.2.2, 1.1.1 • **8:** 0.1.2, 1.3.8	• Interprets and communicates information • Acquires and evaluates information • Allocates money • Allocates material and facility resources • Negotiates • Organizes and maintains information	• Speak so others can understand • Listen actively • Read with understanding • Use math to solve problems and communicate • Observe critically • Guide others

Civics/Lifeskills	Math	Critical Thinking	CASAS	SCANS	EFF Content Standards
• Understand a newspaper ad for an apartment rental • Choose the best neighborhood for you to live in • Seek recommendations for businesses in the community • Complain to your landlord about problems	• Calculate money for rent	• Discern the best businesses in your community • Understand your landlord's responsibilities • Calculate how much you can afford to spend on rent	• **1:** 7.4.5 • **2:** 1.4.1, 1.4.2 • **3:** 1.4.2, 0.1.2, 1.4.3, 1.4.5 • **4:** 1.4.4, 2.2.1, 2.5.4 • **5:** 7.2.1 • **6:** 2.6.4, 1.4.4, 2.1.6, 2.1.8 • **7:** 1.4.7, 1.7.4 • **8:** 1.4.2, 0.1.2	• Negotiates • Acquires and evaluates information • Participates as a member of a team • Interprets and communicates information • Allocates money • Allocates material and facility resources • Allocates time	• Convey ideas in writing • Speak so others can understand • Guide others • Use math to solve problems and communicate • Observe critically • Plan • Solve problems and make decisions • Read with understanding
• Give and follow directions • Obey traffic signs and rules • Practice transacting business at the Department of Motor Vehicles	• Calculating miles and kilometers	• Interpret directions • Understand traffic signs and signals • Draw a map • Recall directions	• **1:** 1.9.2, 2.5.7, 1.9.8, 5.3.6 • **2:** 2.2.1, 2.5.4 • **3:** 1.9.2, 2.5.7, 1.9.8, 5.3.6 • **4:** 7.4.5, 2.2.1, 7.2.1 • **5:** 2.2.1, 2.5.4 • **6:** 2.2.1, 2.5.4 • **7:** 2.2.1, 2.5.4	• Acquires and evaluates information • Understands systems • Participates as a member of a team • Allocates human resources • Teaches others • Negotiates	• Convey ideas in writing • Listen actively • Cooperate with others • Take responsibility for learning • Observe critically • Read with understanding • Use math to solve problems and communicate
• Plan for the immediate future • Schedule leisure activities with friends and family	• Calculating travel time to work	• Choose among several choices for leisure activities • Balance work and personal schedules • Distinguish between plan and possibilities	• **1:** 7.4.5, 0.1.6 • **2:** 0.1.2, 0.2.4, 0.1.4 • **3:** 0.1.2, 0.2.1, 0.2.4 • **4:** 2.3.2, 2.7.1, 7.4.5 • **5:** 2.3.2, 2.7.1 • **6:** 2.6.1, 2.6.2 • **7:** 7.2.1, 7.4.2 • **8:** 4.4.1, 4.4.3, 4.6.5	• Allocates Time • Allocates material and facility resources • Allocates time • Negotiates • Allocates money • Understands systems • Serves clients/customers	• Listen actively • Convey ideas in writing • Cooperate with others • Read with understanding • Reflect and evaluate • Use math to solve problems and communicate
• Plan for the long-term future • Detail the steps to citizenship • Practice applying for enrollment in college	• Calculating to save money for college	• Set personal and professional goals • Describe specific steps to meet your goals	• **1:** 1.9.2, 2.5.7, 7.4.5 • **2:** 0.1.2, 0.2.1 • **3:** 0.1.2, 0.2.4 • **4:** 7.4.5 • **5:** 2.6.4 • **6:** 0.2.2, 0.1.2, 0.2.4 • **7:** 2.5.5	• Interprets and communicates information • Negotiates • Allocates time • Allocates money • Understands systems • Allocates material and facility resources	• Plan • Listen actively • Observe critically • Cooperate with others • Reflect and evaluate • Read with understanding • Use math to solve problems and communicate

PROGRAM OVERVIEW

> **Excellent English: Language Skills for Success** equips students with the grammar and skills they need to access community resources, while developing the foundation for long-term career and academic success.

Excellent English is a four-level, grammar-oriented series for English learners featuring a *Grammar Picture Dictionary* approach to vocabulary building and grammar acquisition. An accessible and predictable sequence of lessons in each unit systematically builds language and math skills around life-skill topics. *Excellent English* is tightly correlated to all of the major standards for adult instruction.

What has led the *Excellent English* team to develop this new series? The program responds to the large and growing need for a new generation of adult materials that provides a more academic alternative to existing publications. *Excellent English* is a natural response to the higher level aspirations of today's adult learners. Stronger reading and writing skills, greater technological proficiency, and a deeper appreciation for today's global economy—increasingly, prospective employees across virtually all industries must exhibit these skill sets to be successful. Interviews with a wide range of administrators, instructors, and students underscore the need for new materials that more quickly prepare students for the vocational and academic challenges they must meet to be successful.

The Complete Excellent English Program

- The **Student Book** features twelve 16-page units that integrate listening, speaking, reading, writing, grammar, math, and pronunciation skills with life-skill topics, critical thinking activities, and civics concepts.

- The **Student Book with Audio Highlights** provides students with audio recordings of all of the Grammar Picture Dictionary, pronunciation, and conversation models in the Student Book.

- The **Workbook with Audio CD** is an essential companion to the Student Book. It provides:
  - Supplementary practice activities correlated to the Student Book.
  - Application lessons that carry vital, standards-based learning objectives through its *Family Connection, Community Connection, Career*

Connection, and *Technology Connection* lessons.
  - Practice tests that encourage students to assess their skills in a low-stakes environment, complete with listening tasks from the Workbook CD.

- The **Teacher's Edition with Tests** provides:
  - Step-by-step procedural notes for each Student Book activity.
  - Expansion activities for the Student Book, many of which offer creative tasks tied to the "big picture" scenes in each unit, including photocopiable worksheets.
  - Culture, Grammar, Academic, Vocabulary, and Pronunciation Notes.
  - A two-page written test for each unit.
  - Audio scripts for audio program materials.
  - Answer keys for Student Book, Workbook, and Tests.

- The **Interactive multimedia program** incorporates and extends the learning goals of the Student Book by integrating language, literacy, and numeracy skill-building with multimedia practice on the computer. A flexible set of activities correlated to each unit builds vocabulary, listening, reading, writing, and test-taking skills.

- The **Color Overhead Transparencies** encourage instructors to present new vocabulary and grammar in fun and meaningful ways. This component provides a full color overhead transparency for each "big picture" scene, as well as transparencies of the grammar charts in each unit.

- The **Big Picture PowerPoint® CD-ROM** includes the "big picture" scenes for all four Student Books. Instructors can use this CD-ROM to project the scenes from a laptop through an LCD or data projector in class.

- The **Audio CDs** and **Audiocassettes** contain recordings for all listening activities in the Student Book. Listening passages for the unit tests are provided on a separate Assessment CD or cassette.

- The **EZ Test® CD-ROM Test Generator** provides a databank of assessment items from which instructors can create customized tests within minutes. The EZ Test assessment materials are also available online at www.eztestonline.com.

Student Book Overview

Consult the *Welcome to Excellent English* guide on pages xiv-xix. This guide offers instructors and administrators a visual tour of one Student Book unit.

Excellent English is designed to maximize accessibility and flexibility. Each unit contains the following sequence of eight, two-page lessons that develop vocabulary and build language, grammar, and math skills around life-skill topics:

- Lesson 1: Grammar and Vocabulary (1)
- Lesson 2: Grammar Practice Plus
- Lesson 3: Listening and Conversation
- Lesson 4: Grammar and Vocabulary (2)
- Lesson 5: Grammar Practice Plus
- Lesson 6: Apply Your Knowledge
- Lesson 7: Reading and Writing
- Lesson 8: Career Connection and Check Your Progress

Each lesson in *Excellent English* is designed as a two-page spread. Lessons 1 and 4 introduce new grammar points and vocabulary sets that allow students to practice the grammar in controlled and meaningful ways. Lessons 2 and 5—the Grammar Practice Plus lessons—provide more opened-ended opportunities for students to use their new language productively. Lesson 3 allows students to hear a variety of listening inputs and to use their new language skills in conversation. Lesson 6 provides an opportunity for students to integrate all their language skills in a real-life application. In Lesson 7, students develop the more academic skills of reading and writing through explicit teaching of academic strategies and exposure to multiple text types and writing tasks. Each unit ends with Lesson 8, an exciting capstone that offers both Career Connection—a compelling "photo story" episode underscoring the vocational objectives of the series—and Check Your Progress—a self-evaluation task. Each lesson addresses a key adult standard, and these standards are indicated in the scope and sequence and in the footer at the bottom of the left-hand page in each lesson.

SPECIAL FEATURES IN EACH STUDENT BOOK UNIT

- **Grammar Picture Dictionary**. Lessons 1 and 4 introduce students to vocabulary and grammar through a picture dictionary approach. This context-rich approach allows students to acquire grammatical structures as they build vocabulary.

- **Grammar Charts**. Also in Lessons 1 and 4, new grammar points are presented in clear paradigms, providing easy reference for students and instructors.

- **"Grammar Professor" Notes**. Additional information related to key grammar points is provided at point of use through the "Grammar Professor" feature. A cheerful, red-haired character appears next to each of these additional grammar points, calling students' attention to learning points in an inviting and memorable way.

- **Math**. Learning basic math skills is critically important for success in school, on the job, and at home. As such, national and state standards for adult education mandate instruction in basic math skills. In each unit, a Math box is dedicated to helping students develop the functional numeracy skills they need for success with basic math.

- **Pronunciation**. This special feature has two major goals: (1) helping students hear and produce specific sounds, words, and minimal pairs of words so they become better listeners and speakers; and (2) addressing issues of stress, rhythm, and intonation so that students' spoken English becomes more comprehensible.

- *What about you?* Throughout each unit of the Student Book, students are encouraged to apply new language to their own lives through personalization activities.

- **"Big Picture" scenes**. Lesson 2 in each unit introduces a "big picture" scene. This scene serves as a springboard to a variety of activities provided in the Student Book, Teacher's Edition, Color Overhead Transparencies package and the Big Picture PowerPoint CD-ROM. In the Student Book, the "big picture" scene features key vocabulary and serves as a prompt for language activities that practice the grammar points of the unit. The scene features characters with distinct personalities for students to enjoy, respond to, and talk about.

- **Career-themed "photo story"**. Each unit ends with a compelling "photo story" episode. These four-panel scenes feature chapters in the life of an adult working to take the next step in his or her professional future. In Book 1, we follow Isabel as she identifies the next step she'd like to take in her career and works to get the education and training she needs to move ahead. The engaging photo story format provides students with role models as they pursue their own career and academic goals.

CIVICS CONCEPTS

Many institutions focus direct attention on the importance of civics instruction for English language learners. Civics instruction encourages students to become active and informed community members. The Teacher's Edition includes multiple *Community Connection* activities in each unit. These activities encourage learners to become more active and informed members of their communities.

ACADEMIC SKILL DEVELOPMENT

Many adult programs recognize the need to help students develop important academic skills that will facilitate lifelong learning. The *Excellent English* Student Book addresses this need through explicit teaching of reading and writing strategies, explicit presentation and practice of grammar, and academic notes in the Teacher's Edition. The Teacher's Edition also includes multiple *Academic Connection* activities in each unit. These activities encourage learners to become more successful in an academic environment.

CASAS, SCANS, EFF, AND OTHER STANDARDS

Instructors and administrators benchmark student progress against national and/or state standards for adult instruction. With this in mind, *Excellent English* carefully integrates instructional elements from a wide range of standards including CASAS, SCANS, EFF, TABE CLAS-E, the Florida Adult ESOL Syllabi, and the Los Angeles Unified School District Course Outlines. Unit-by-unit correlations of some of these standards appear in the Student Book scope and sequence on pages iv-ix. Other correlations appear in the Teacher's Edition. Here is a brief overview of our approach to meeting the key national and state standards:

- **CASAS**. Many U.S. states, including California, tie funding for adult education programs to student performance on the Comprehensive Adult Student Assessment System (CASAS). The CASAS (www.casas. org) competencies identify more than 30 essential skills that adults need in order to succeed in the classroom, workplace, and community. *Excellent English* comprehensively integrates all of the CASAS Life Skill Competencies throughout the four levels of the series.

- **SCANS**. Developed by the United States Department of Labor, SCANS is an acronym for the Secretary's Commission on Achieving Necessary Skills (wdr.doleta. gov/SCANS/). SCANS competencies are workplace skills that help people compete more effectively in today's global economy. A variety of SCANS competencies is threaded throughout the activities in each unit of *Excellent English*. The incorporation

of these competencies recognizes both the intrinsic importance of teaching workplace skills and the fact that many adult students are already working members of their communities.

- **EFF**. Equipped for the Future (EFF) is a set of standards for adult literacy and lifelong learning, developed by The National Institute for Literacy (www. nifl.gov). The organizing principle of EFF is that adults assume responsibilities in three major areas of life – as workers, as parents, and as citizens. These three areas of focus are called "role maps" in the EFF documentation. Each *Excellent English* unit addresses all three of the EFF role maps in the Student Book or Workbook.

- **Florida Adult ESOL Syllabi** provide the curriculum frameworks for all six levels of instruction; Foundations, Low Beginning, High Beginning, Low Intermediate, High Intermediate, and Advanced. The syllabi were developed by the State of Florida as a guide to include the following areas of adult literacy standards: workplace, communication (listen, speak, read, and write), technology, interpersonal communication, health and nutrition, government and community resources, consumer education, family and parenting, concepts of time and money, safety and security, and language development (grammar and pronunciation). *Excellent English* Level 1 incorporates into its instruction the vast majority of standards at the Low Beginning level.

- **TABE Complete Language Assessment System— English (CLAS-E)** has been developed by CTB/ McGraw-Hill and provides administrators and teachers with accurate, reliable evaluations of adult students' English language skills. TABE CLAS-E measures students' reading, listening, writing, and speaking skills at all English proficiency levels and also assesses critically important grammar standards. TABE CLAS-E scores are linked to TABE 9 and 10, providing a battery of assessment tools that offer seamless transition from English language to adult basic education assessment.

- **Los Angeles Unified School District (LAUSD) Course Outlines**. LAUSD Competency-Based Education (CBE) Course Outlines were developed to guide teachers in lesson planning and to inform students about what they will be able to do after successful completion of their course. The CBE Course outlines focus on acquiring skills in listening, speaking, reading and writing in the context of everyday life. *Excellent English* addresses all four language skills in the contexts of home, community and work, appropriately targeting Beginning Low adult ESL students.

TECHNOLOGY

Technology plays an increasingly important role in our lives as students, workers, family members, and citizens. Every unit in the Workbook includes a two-page lesson titled *Technology Connection* that focuses on some aspect of technology in our everyday lives.

Administrators and instructors are encouraged to incorporate interactive tasks from the *Excellent English* Multimedia Program into classroom and/or lab use as this package includes hours of meaningful technology-based practice of all key Student Book objectives.

The EZ Test® CD-ROM Test Generator—and its online version, available at www.eztestonline.com—allow instructors to easily create customized tests from a digital databank of assessment items.

NUMBER OF HOURS OF INSTRUCTION

The *Excellent English* program has been designed to accommodate the needs of adult classes with 80-180 hours of classroom instruction. Here are three recommended ways in which various components in the *Excellent English* program can be combined to meet student and instructor needs.

- **80-100 hours**. Instructors are encouraged to work through all of the Student Book materials. The Color Overhead Transparencies can be used to introduce and/or review materials in each unit. Instructors should also look to the Teacher's Edition for teaching suggestions and testing materials as necessary. *Time per unit: 8-10 hours.*

- **100-140 hours**. In addition to working through all of the Student Book materials, instructors are encouraged to incorporate the Workbook and the interactive multimedia activities for supplementary practice. *Time per unit: 10-14 hours.*

- **140-180 hours**. Instructors and students working in an intensive instructional setting can take advantage of the wealth of expansion activities threaded through the Teacher's Edition to supplement the Student Book, Workbook, and interactive multimedia materials. *Time per unit: 14-18 hours.*

ASSESSMENT

The *Excellent English* program offers instructors, students, and administrators the following wealth of resources for monitoring and assessing student progress and achievement:

- **Standardized testing formats**. *Excellent English* is comprehensively correlated to the CASAS competencies and all of the other major national and state standards for adult learning. Students have the opportunity to practice answering CASAS-style listening questions in Lessons 3 or 6 of each Student Book unit, and both listening and reading questions in the Unit tests in the Teacher's Edition and practice tests in the Workbook. Students practice with the same items types and bubble-in answer sheets they encounter on CASAS and other standardized tests.

- **Achievement tests**. The *Excellent English* Teacher's Edition includes paper-and-pencil end-of-unit tests. In addition, the *EZ Test® CD-ROM Test Generator* provides a databank of assessment items from which instructors can create customized tests within minutes. The EZ Test assessment materials are also available online at www.eztestonline.com. These tests help students demonstrate how well they have learned the instructional content of the unit. Adult learners often show incremental increases in learning that are not always measured on the standardized tests. The achievement tests may demonstrate learning even in a short amount of instructional time. Twenty percent of each test includes questions that encourage students to apply more academic skills such as determining meaning from context, making inferences, and understanding main ideas. Practice with these question types will help prepare students who may want to enroll in academic classes.

- **Performance-based assessment**. *Excellent English* provides several ways to measure students' performance on productive tasks, including the Writing tasks in Lesson 7 of each Student Book unit. In addition, the Teacher's Edition suggests writing and speaking prompts that instructors can use for performance-based assessment.

- **Portfolio assessment**. A portfolio is a collection of student work that can be used to show progress. Examples of work that the instructor or the student may submit in the portfolio include writing samples, speaking rubrics, audiotapes, videotapes, or projects.

- **Self-assessment**. Self-assessment is an important part of the overall assessment picture, as it promotes student involvement and commitment to the learning process. When encouraged to assess themselves, students take more control of their learning and are better able to connect the instructional content with their own goals. The Student Book includes Check Your Progress activities at the end of each unit, which allow students to assess their knowledge of vocabulary and grammar. Students can chart their mastery of the key language lessons in the unit, and use this information to set new learning goals.

Welcome to Excellent English!

Grammar Picture Dictionary uses engaging illustrations to showcase target grammar and vocabulary.

Clear and thorough **grammar charts** make target grammar points accessible and easily comprehensible.

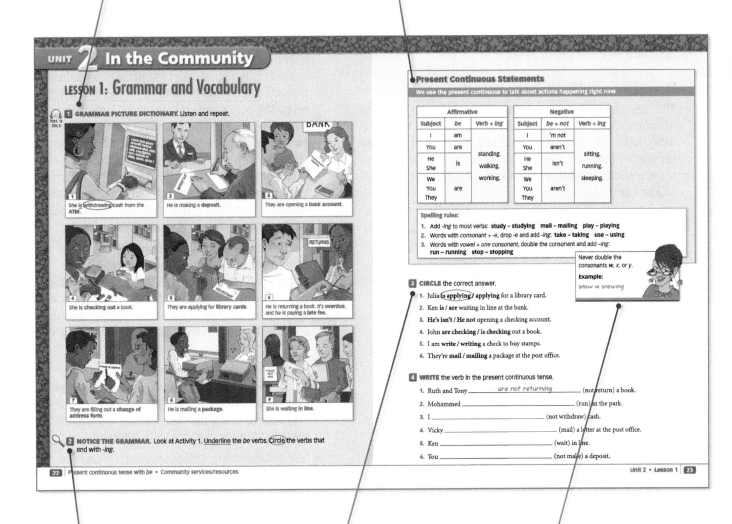

Notice the Grammar activities make students aware of the form and function of new grammar points.

Scaffolded grammar activities systematically expose, stress, and review each key grammar structure.

A Grammar Professor calls students' attention to additional grammar points in an inviting and memorable way.

Big Picture activities provide rich opportunities for classroom discussion and practice with new language.

LESSON 2: Grammar Practice Plus

Present Continuous Questions

Yes/No Questions

Be	Subject	Verb + ing
Am	I	
Are	you	learning? waiting? working?
Is	he she	
Are	we you they	

Answers

	Subject	Verb
Yes,	I	am.
	you	are.
	he she	is.
	you they	are.

	Subject	Verb + not
No,	I	'm not.
	you	aren't.
	he she	isn't.
	you they	aren't.

Information Questions

Question Word	be	Subject	Verb + ing
What	are	you	doing?
Where	is	he	going?
Why	is	the bank	closing?

Answers

I'm making a deposit.
To the library.
Because it is 5:00.

1 WRITE. Complete the sentences. Then match the questions with the answers.

_c_ 1. Why ___is he paying___ (he/pay) a late fee?   a. Yes, I am.

___ 2. _____ (you/buy) stamps?   b. No, they aren't.

___ 3. _____ (they/make) a deposit?   c. Because his book is overdue.

___ 4. What _____ (you/do)?   d. At the library.

___ 5. Where _____ (she/study)?   e. We're filling out forms.

2 WHAT ABOUT YOU? Look around your classroom. Answer the questions.

1. What is the teacher doing? _____

2. Is the teacher speaking? _____

3. What are the students doing? _____

4. Are the students listening to the teacher? _____

3 TALK about the picture.

The people are at a mall.

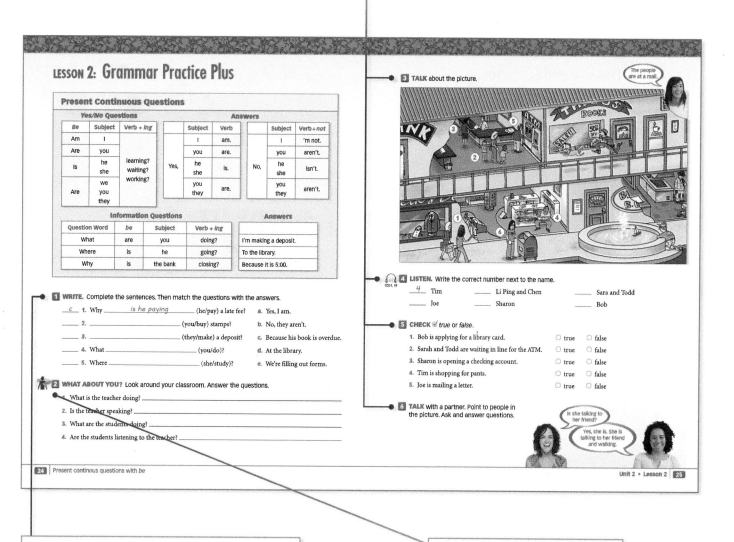

4 LISTEN. Write the correct number next to the name. *[CD1, 19]*

_4_ Tim   ___ Li Ping and Chen   ___ Sara and Todd

___ Joe   ___ Sharon   ___ Bob

5 CHECK ☑ true or false.

1. Bob is applying for a library card.   ☐ true ☐ false

2. Sarah and Todd are waiting in line for the ATM.   ☐ true ☐ false

3. Sharon is opening a checking account.   ☐ true ☐ false

4. Tim is shopping for pants.   ☐ true ☐ false

5. Joe is mailing a letter.   ☐ true ☐ false

6 TALK with a partner. Point to people in the picture. Ask and answer questions.

Is she talking to her friend?

Yes, she is. She is talking to her friend and walking.

Grammar Practice Plus lessons introduce additional vocabulary while recycling and practicing the target grammar.

Personalization activities encourage students to use new grammar to talk about their own experiences.

Listening comprehension activities provide students with opportunities to build practical listening skills.

Life skills-based listening activities integrate grammar and vocabulary to provide students with models of everyday conversation.

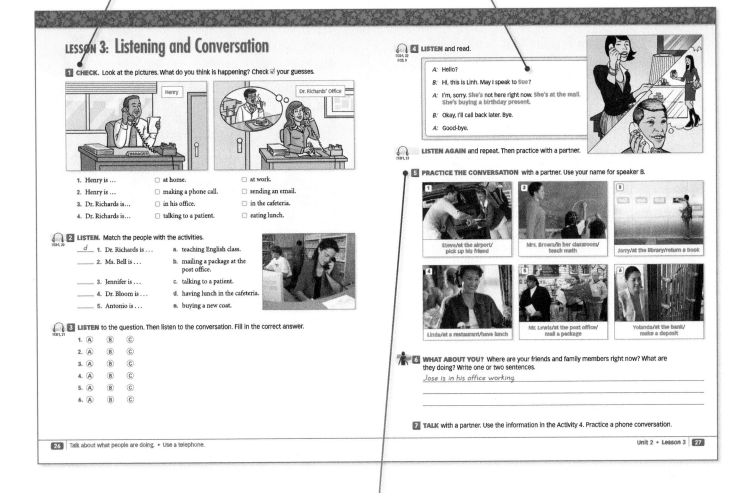

LESSON 3: Listening and Conversation

1 CHECK. Look at the pictures. What do you think is happening? Check ☑ your guesses.

Henry

Dr. Richards' Office

1. Henry is …	☐ at home.	☐ at work.
2. Henry is …	☐ making a phone call.	☐ sending an email.
3. Dr. Richards is…	☐ in his office.	☐ in the cafeteria.
4. Dr. Richards is…	☐ talking to a patient.	☐ eating lunch.

2 LISTEN. Match the people with the activities.
TCD1, 20

_d_ 1. Dr. Richards is …   a. teaching English class.

___ 2. Ms. Bell is …   b. mailing a package at the post office.

___ 3. Jennifer is …   c. talking to a patient.

___ 4. Dr. Bloom is …   d. having lunch in the cafeteria.

___ 5. Antonio is …   e. buying a new coat.

3 LISTEN to the question. Then listen to the conversation. Fill in the correct answer.
TCD1, 21

1. Ⓐ   Ⓑ   Ⓒ
2. Ⓐ   Ⓑ   Ⓒ
3. Ⓐ   Ⓑ   Ⓒ
4. Ⓐ   Ⓑ   Ⓒ
5. Ⓐ   Ⓑ   Ⓒ
6. Ⓐ   Ⓑ   Ⓒ

4 LISTEN and read.
TCD1, 22
3 CD, 9

A: Hello?

B: Hi, this is Linh. May I speak to Sue?

A: I'm, sorry. She's not here right now. She's at the mall. She's buying a birthday present.

B: Okay, I'll call back later. Bye.

A: Good-bye.

LISTEN AGAIN and repeat. Then practice with a partner.
TCD1, 23

5 PRACTICE THE CONVERSATION with a partner. Use your name for speaker B.

1. Steve/at the airport/ pick up his friend
2. Mrs. Brown/in her classroom/ teach math
3. Jerry/at the library/return a book
4. Linda/at a restaurant/have lunch
5. Mr. Lewis/at the post office/ mail a package
6. Yolanda/at the bank/ make a deposit

6 WHAT ABOUT YOU? Where are your friends and family members right now? What are they doing? Write one or two sentences.

Jose is in his office working.

_____

_____

7 TALK with a partner. Use the information in the Activity 4. Practice a phone conversation.

Guided speaking activities provide controlled practice of new grammar and vocabulary while building students' confidence with the target language.

Apply Your Knowledge lessons provide students with opportunities to practice listening, speaking, reading, and writing skills in real-world situations.

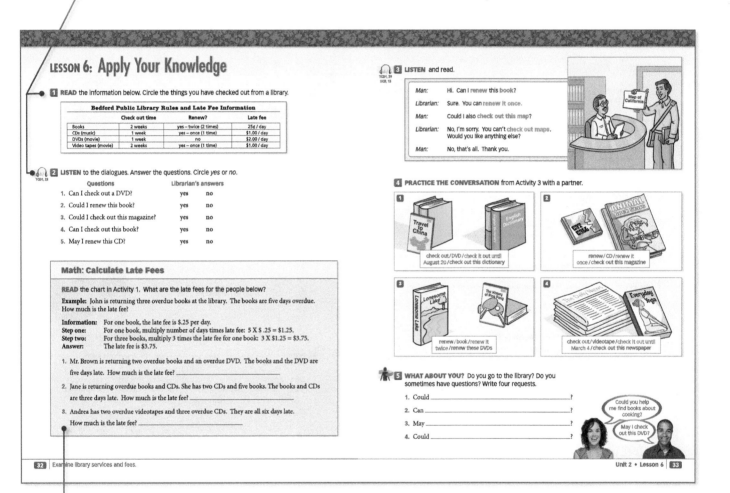

LESSON 6: Apply Your Knowledge

1 READ the information below. Circle the things you have checked out from a library.

Bedford Public Library Rules and Late Fee Information

	Check out time	Renew?	Late fee
Books	2 weeks	yes – twice (2 times)	25¢ / day
CDs (music)	1 week	yes – once (1 time)	$1.00 / day
DVDs (movie)	1 week	no	$2.00 / day
Video tapes (movie)	2 weeks	yes – once (1 time)	$1.00 / day

2 LISTEN to the dialogues. Answer the questions. Circle *yes* or *no*.

Questions	Librarian's answers	
1. Can I check out a DVD?	yes	no
2. Could I renew this book?	yes	no
3. Could I check out this magazine?	yes	no
4. Can I check out this book?	yes	no
5. May I renew this CD?	yes	no

Math: Calculate Late Fees

READ the chart in Activity 1. What are the late fees for the people below?

Example: John is returning three overdue books at the library. The books are five days overdue. How much is the late fee?

Information: For one book, the late fee is $.25 per day.
Step one: For one book, multiply number of days times late fee: 5 X $ .25 = $1.25.
Step two: For three books, multiply 3 times the late fee for one book: 3 X $1.25 = $3.75.
Answer: The late fee is $3.75.

1. Mr. Brown is returning two overdue books and an overdue DVD. The books and the DVD are five days late. How much is the late fee? _____

2. Jane is returning overdue books and CDs. She has two CDs and five books. The books and CDs are three days late. How much is the late fee? _____

3. Andrea has two overdue videotapes and three overdue CDs. They are all six days late. How much is the late fee? _____

3 LISTEN and read.

Man:	Hi. Can I renew this book?
Librarian:	Sure. You can renew it once.
Man:	Could I also check out this map?
Librarian:	No, I'm sorry. You can't check out maps. Would you like anything else?
Man:	No, that's all. Thank you.

4 PRACTICE THE CONVERSATION from Activity 3 with a partner.

1. check out/DVD/check it out until August 20/check out this dictionary

2. renew/CD/renew it once/check out this magazine

3. renew/book/renew it twice/renew these DVDs

4. check out/videotape/check it out until March 4/check out this newspaper

5 WHAT ABOUT YOU? Do you go to the library? Do you sometimes have questions? Write four requests.

1. Could _____?
2. Can _____?
3. May _____?
4. Could _____?

Could you help me find books about cooking?

May I check out this DVD?

Math activities allow students to apply newly acquired vocabulary and grammar in a specific academic content area.

Pre-reading tasks activate prior knowledge and introduce the reading passage.

A series of **highly-scaffolded tasks** culminates in an academic or practical writing task.

Reading and Writing Tips help students develop critical academic skills.

LESSON 7: Reading

1 THINK ABOUT IT. Do you send and receive email? Do you send and receive letters? Do you send and receive text messages?

2 BEFORE YOU READ. Scan the email. Circle the date, who the message is to, and who the message is from.

Reading Tip

Before you read an email, quickly **scan** the message. Look for (1) the day or date of the message, (2) who the message is from, and (3) who the message is to.

3 READ. Underline the activities (present continuous verbs) in the email.

FROM: Martha Thomas
TO: Sam Johnson
SENT: April 4, 3:30 PM
SUBJECT: Hi

Hi Sam,

How are you? I'm thinking about you! What are you doing? Of course, I know the answer. You're reading this message on your computer!

I am relaxing in my bedroom and writing you this note. My family isn't relaxing. My mother is cleaning the house. My father is at the mall. He is exchanging some clothes. My sister is at the bank. She's opening an account. They are all very busy.

How are you? How is your new job? How is your new apartment? Could you send me some photos? Write me soon!

Martha

4 ANSWER the question. Circle the main idea of the email.

a. Martha is busy, and her family is busy, too.
b. Martha is relaxing, but her family is busy.
c. Martha and Sam are friends.

5 EDIT. Cross out the mistakes in the sentences. Write the correct words.

1. Martha's mother is cleaning the car. *house*
2. Martha is studying in her bedroom.
3. Her father is at work.
4. He is buying some things.
5. Martha's sister is closing a bank account.
6. Martha's sister is at the mall.

Writing

1 EDIT the email. Add periods, question marks, capital letters, and commas.

Writing Tip

When we write an informal note or email to a friend, we start with a **greeting**. There is always a comma after the greeting.
Example: Hi George,

Check mail   Compose   Search mail   Search Web

(1) Inbox
    Draft
(2) Sent
    Bulk
    Trash

G
dear george

how are you i'm using the computer at the library the library is a

busy place many people are reading   some students are taking a

computer class the teacher is helping the students   my friend is

here with me she is studying her English

lesson many people are looking for books

this is a nice library I like to come here

could you write to me soon

mary

2 WRITE a note to a friend. Write about your classmates or family members and the activities they are doing right now.

_____
_____
_____
_____
_____

3 EDIT your note for capital letters, question marks, commas, and periods.

Reading comprehension activities allow students to exercise their understanding of new content and grammar.

Reading passages provide students with community- or school- based texts they will encounter in daily life.

Career-themed photo story provides students with role models for improving their educational and/or career prospects.

Check Your Progress ensures student comprehension and retention of each unit's target grammar and vocabulary.

Career Connection

1 READ AND LISTEN. Then practice with a partner.

1. Look, Oscar, the manager's job is on the board.

Really? That's great, Eric!

2. "Strong leadership skills. Computer skills necessary." Hmm.

3. How can I learn computer skills in two or three weeks?

Well, you can check out a book about computers from the library. Or you can take a class at night school.

4. Good idea, Eric! I'll look at the class schedule tonight.

I'm taking a cooking class right now. You can learn a lot in a few weeks.

2 CHECK ☑ yes or no.

1. The manager's job is posted on the job board. ☐ yes ☐ no
2. Oscar has computer skills. ☐ yes ☐ no
3. The library has books about computers. ☐ yes ☐ no
4. Eric is taking a cooking class now. ☐ yes ☐ no

3 WHAT ABOUT YOU? Can you use a computer? Can you cook? What new skills do you want to learn?

Check Your Progress!

Skill	Circle the answers.	Is it correct?
A. Make present continuous statements.	1. Bob **is makes/is making** a deposit. 2. Maria **is checking out/checking out** a book. 3. David and Linda **is returning/are returning** a book. 4. He **isn't waiting/doesn't waiting** in line.	☐ ☐ ☐ ☐

Number Correct 0 1 2 3 4

Skill	Circle the answers.	Is it correct?
B. Make present continuous questions.	5. **What/Where** are they going? To the library. 6. **Why/What** is he paying a late fee? Because the book is overdue. 7. Where **is/are** Mike and Linda studying? At Linda's house. 8. Are Sue and Lee mailing a package? **No they aren't./Yes, she is.**	☐ ☐ ☐ ☐

Number Correct 0 1 2 3 4

Skill	Circle the answers.	Is it correct?
C. Make polite requests at the store.	9. **Would/Could** I exchange this shirt? 10. **Would/Why** you like a plastic or paper bag? 11. **May/Would** I return these shoes. 12. **Would/Can** I use this coupon?	☐ ☐ ☐ ☐

Number Correct 0 1 2 3 4

Skill	Circle the answers.	Is it correct?
D. Use the library.	13. How much is the late fee? **It's $1.50/It's two days.** 14. I'm paying a late fee because the DVD is **renew/overdue.** 15. I'm sorry you can't **overdue/check out** newspapers. 16. I want the book for one more week. May I **renew/late fee** it?	☐ ☐ ☐ ☐

Number Correct 0 1 2 3 4

COUNT the number of correct answers above. Fill in the circles.

Chart Your Success					
Skill	Needs Practice	Needs Practice	Okay	Very Good	Excellent!
A. Make present continuous statements.	⓪	①	②	③	④
B. Make present continuous questions.	⓪	①	②	③	④
C. Make polite requests at the store.	⓪	①	②	③	④
D. Use the library.	⓪	①	②	③	④

Useful Language

1 **LISTEN** and repeat the letters.

Aa	Bb	Cc	Dd	Ee	Ff	Gg	Hh	Ii	Jj	Kk	Ll	Mm
Nn	Oo	Pp	Qq	Rr	Ss	Tt	Uu	Vv	Ww	Xx	Yy	Zz

2 **LISTEN** and read.

A: Hi, I'm Suzy Lee.

B: It's nice to meet you Suzy. I'm Marta.

A: How do you spell your name?

B: M-A-R-T-A.

A: Where are you from, Marta?

B: I'm from Cuba. And you?

A: I'm from China.

LISTEN AGAIN and repeat.

3 **TALK** with five classmates. Complete the chart.

First name	Country
Suzy	China
1.	
2.	
3.	
4.	
5.	

4 **TALK.** Introduce a classmate.

This is Suzy. She's from China.

5 **MONTHS.** Write the missing letters.

1. Jan _u_ a _r_ y
2. Febr ___ ar ___
3. ___ arch
4. A ___ ril
5. ___ ay
6. Ju ___ e

7. ___ uly
8. Au ___ u ___ t
9. Se ___ tem ___ er
10. O ___ tobe ___
11. ___ ove ___ ber
12. De ___ emb ___ r

When is your birthday?

December 20th.

6 **TALK** with your classmates. Write the information.

Classmate's name	Birthday
Maria	*December 20th*
1.	
2.	
3.	

7 **MATCH** the questions and answers.

___c___ 1. What does *excellent* mean?

_____ 2. Is my answer correct?

_____ 3. How do you spell *Florida*?

_____ 4. Can you repeat that?

_____ 5. May I work with you?

_____ 6. Could I borrow your pencil?

a. Yes, your answer is correct!

b. I said, "The address is 293 Elm Street."

c. *Excellent* means very, very good.

d. Sure. I'd like to work with you.

e. Yes, of course. You can borrow my pencil.

f. F-L-O-R-I-D-A.

TCD1, 5

LISTEN. Are your answers correct?

8 **TALK.** Practice the questions in Activity 7 and answers with a partner.

Grammar

1 **NOUNS.** A noun is a person, place or thing. (Circle) the nouns.

1. My (teacher) is nice.
2. San Diego is beautiful.
3. My car is new.
4. Sam is tall.

5. The windows are clean.
6. Are the children noisy?
7. Maria is absent today.
8. The United States is large.

2 **PRONOUNS.** We use pronouns in place of nouns. Underline the pronouns.

1. My father is a doctor. <u>He</u> is 49 years old.
2. My mother is working right now. She works at a hospital.
3. My school is on Elm Street. It is next to the library.
4. My name is Mary. I am a student.
5. Sue and Mike are my classmates. They are very nice.
6. The houses on my street are small, but they are very nice.

3 **ADJECTIVES.** Adjectives describe nouns and pronouns. (Circle) the adjectives.

1. The (blue) car is (dirty)
2. The green books are on the white table.
3. I am tired.

4. The small boy is eating a big apple.
5. She is tall and pretty.
6. He is short and thin.

4 **WRITE** sentences under the pictures. Use a pronoun, *is* or *are* and a word from the box.

| old | young | clean | happy |

It is clean.

5 VERBS. Verbs are actions. Circle the verbs.

1. He dances very well.
2. I speak Spanish.
3. I worked yesterday.
4. She watches T.V. at night.

5. He walks to school every day.
6. He is listening to music right now.
7. They eat lunch at 12:00.
8. My children play soccer every Saturday.

6 BE is also a verb. It is not an action verb. Circle the *be* verbs.

1. My name is Henri.
2. You are a good student.
3. It is nice to meet you.
4. We were absent yesterday.

5. I was sick yesterday.
6. I am happy today.
7. They are good students.
8. She isn't tall.

7 PUNCTUATION. Read the story. Answer the questions.

My name is Alina Perez. I live in Dallas, Texas. I go to English class on Tuesdays, Wednesdays, and Thursdays. My teacher's name is Joy Miller. I like my teacher!

Punctuation	
Capital letters	**A, B, C**
Small letters	**a, b, c**
Period	**.**
Comma	**,**
Question mark	**?**
Exclamation mark	**!**

1. How many capital letters are in the story? _____

2. How many periods are there? _____

3. How many commas are there? _____

4. How many question marks are there? _____

5. How many exclamation marks are there? _____

LESSON 1: Grammar and Vocabulary

1 GRAMMAR PICTURE DICTIONARY. Listen and repeat.

TCD1, 6
SCD, 2

1
My wife and I have three children. They are all **adults**.

2
Our son and **daughter-in-law** have one son.

3
Our daughter-in-law is **pregnant**.

4
Our older daughter is **divorced**.

5
She has **twins**.

6
Our younger daughter is **engaged**.

7
My mother-in-law is 83 years old. She is **widowed**.

8
Our grandson is eight years old. His **cousins** are five years old.

9
We are **proud** parents and grandparents.

2 NOTICE THE GRAMMAR. Look at Activity 1. Underline the *be* verbs. Circle *have* and *has*.

> There are two kinds of **negative contractions** with *be*. *He's not.* = *He isn't.*

Present Tense of *Be*

We use *be* when we describe people and relationships.

Affirmative

Subject	*be*	
I	am	divorced.
You	are	engaged.
He She	is	my cousin.
We You They	are	40 years old.

Negative

Subject	*be*	*not*	
I	am	not	married.
You	are	not	single.
He She	is	not	my twin.
We You They	are	not	30 years old.

Contractions

I am = I'm
You are = You're
He is = He's
She is = She's
We are = We're
They are = They're

Contractions

I am not = I'm not
You are not = You're not/You aren't
He is not = He's not/He isn't
She is not = She's not/She isn't
We are not = We're not/We aren't
They are not = They're not/They aren't

---

3 **WRITE.** Complete the sentences. Use the correct affirmative or negative form of the verb *be*.

1. Mr. and Mrs. Garcia have a daughter. She _____*is*_____ twelve years old.

2. Lisa _____ married. She's single.

3. Jacob and Nat _____ cousins. They're twins!

4. Susan _____ pregnant. She and her husband _____ very happy.

5. Bob and Mary _____ engaged. The wedding date _____ July 12.

6. I _____ married. I'm divorced.

7. My husband and I have two grandchildren. Our granddaughter _____ 14 years old.

8. We _____ proud of our grandchildren.

4 **WHAT ABOUT YOU?** In your notebook, draw a picture of your family. Then tell a classmate about your family.

> This is my grandmother. Her name is Elizabeth. She...

LESSON 2: Grammar Practice Plus

1 WRITE the numbers next to the words.

__4__ a beard

_____ a mustache

_____ curly brown hair

_____ wavy blonde hair

_____ straight black hair

_____ freckles

_____ glasses

2 WRITE. Complete the paragraph. Use the correct form of *be* or *have*.

I ___*have*___ three children. They ___*are*___
       1   2
all very different. My older son ___*is*___ 23 years old.
                                      3
He _____ tall and thin. He _____ curly
         4   5
brown hair and brown eyes. My daughter _____
                                              6
18 years old. She _____ short and thin. She
                        7
_____ wavy blonde hair. She also _____
         8   9
glasses. My younger son _____ 16 years old. He
                             10
_____ tall and heavy. He _____ short,
        11   12
straight black hair. He also _____ freckles. My children
                                  13
look very different, but they _____ all very attractive!
                                   14

Describing people	
have	*be*
a beard	tall
a mustache	short
glasses	thin
freckles	heavy
blonde hair	12 years old
brown eyes	attractive
long hair	

He **has** a beard.
They **are** attractive.

3 WRITE. Describe a classmate. Write four sentences.

Example: ___*He*___ is ___*tall*___ .

1. _____ is _____ .

2. _____ is _____ .

3. _____ has _____ .

4. _____ has _____ .

4 **TALK** about the picture. What is the special day? Who are the people?

This is the father.

Clara

5 **LISTEN.** Write the names on the picture.

TCD1, 7

Clara	Jose	Laura	Sofia	Pablo

6 **WRITE.** One word in each sentence is not correct. Find the word. Write the sentences correctly.

1. Clara is 2̶5̶ years old. _____Clara is 7 years old._____

2. Pablo has a beard. _____

3. Jose has short blonde hair. _____

4. Sofia has wavy hair. _____

5. Laura is pregnant. _____

7 **TALK** with a partner. Describe a person in the picture. Your partner guesses the person.

She has brown hair and brown eyes. She's seven years old.

Is it Clara?

Yes!

LESSON 3: Listening and Conversation

1 **LISTEN** to the question. Then listen to the announcement. Fill in the correct answer.

1. Ⓐ　Ⓑ　Ⓒ
2. Ⓐ　Ⓑ　Ⓒ
3. Ⓐ　Ⓑ　Ⓒ
4. Ⓐ　Ⓑ　Ⓒ

2 **LISTEN AGAIN.** Number the pictures.

Math: Calculate Ages

WRITE. Answer the questions.

1. Tom's birthdate is September 6, 1982. How old is he?

   He is 26 years old.

2. The Brown family has twin boys. Their birthdate is August 10, 2003. How old are they?

   _____

3. Maria's birthdate is February 1, 1970. How old is she now?

   _____

4. Today is Diana's birthday. She was born in 1946. How old is she?

   _____

5. Today is Suzy's birthday. She is 12. What is her birthdate?

   _____

TCD1, 10
SCD, 3

3 **LISTEN** and read.

A: I'm looking for my wife.

B: What does she look like?

A: She's tall and thin. She has straight black hair.

B: There she is.

A: Oh, thank you!

TCD1, 11 **LISTEN AGAIN** and repeat. Then practice with a partner.

4 **PRACTICE THE CONVERSATION** with a partner.

1. grandfather

3. sister

2. son

4. mother

5. granddaughter

6. brother-in-law

5 **WHAT ABOUT YOU?** Talk with a partner. Describe a classmate. Your partner points to the classmate.

A: I'm looking for my friend.

B: What does she look like?

A: She's young. She's short and thin. She has brown hair and glasses.

B: There she is.

A: Thank you.

LESSON 4: Grammar and Vocabulary

1 **GRAMMAR PICTURE DICTIONARY.** Listen and repeat.

1

A: Is she in **preschool**?
B: Yes, she is.

2

A: Is he in **elementary school**?
B: Yes, he is.

3

A: Are they in elementary school?
B: No, they aren't. They're in **high school**.

4

A: Are you in **college**?
B: Yes, I am.

5

A: What is the **custodian's** name?
B: His name is Joe Benson.

6

A: Where are the students?
B: They are in the **principal's** office.

7

A: Who is the **school counselor**?
B: It's Ms. Smith.

Spencer High School

The school will be closed from December 16th until January 2nd.

Please make sure that you empty your lockers of all your school supplies.

8

A: When is the **winter vacation**?
B: It's December 16 to January 2.

2 **NOTICE THE GRAMMAR.** Look at Activity 1. Circle the *be* verbs.

Questions with *Be*

Yes/No Questions

Be	Subject	
Am	I	a student?
Are	you	
Is	he	
Are	we they	in high school?

Answers

	Subject	be
Yes,	you	are.
	I	am.
	he	is.
	you they	are.

	Subject	be
No,	you	are not.
	I	am not.
	he	is not.
	you they	are not.

Information Questions

Question Word	be	Subject
What	is	his name?
Where	is	she?
When	is	his birthday?
Who	are	they?

Answers

Subject	be	
His name	is	Pedro.
She	is	at school.
It	is	May 4.
They	are	my sisters.

3 **MATCH** the questions with the answers.

_b_ 1. Who is the principal?

_____ 2. Is he in preschool?

_____ 3. Where are the teachers?

_____ 4. When is the starting date?

_____ 5. Are they students?

_____ 6. What are your sons' names?

a. Yes, he is.

b. It's David Gomez.

c. It's August 29.

d. Yes, they are.

e. They are in their classrooms.

f. Their names are Bob and Jim.

4 **WHAT ABOUT YOU?** Answer the questions.

1. Are you a student? _____

2. Who is your teacher? _____

3. What is the name of your school? _____

4. When is the spring vacation at your school? _____

5. What is your school's address? _____

LESSON 5: Grammar Practice Plus

1 **READ.** Look at the chart about public schools in Spencer City.

	Name of School	Education/ Grade level	Contact Person	Address
Preschool	Greenhouse Pre-school	Childcare for children 3-5 years old	Mr. Todd Jackson, Director	50 Main Street
Primary Schools	Kennedy Elementary School	Kindergarten – 5th grade	Ms. Carol Pho, Principal	11 Elm Street
	Main Street School	Kindergarten – 3rd grade	Mr. Todd Jackson, Principal	50 Main Street
	Wayne Elementary School	4th – 6th grade	Mr. Miguel Rosa, Principal	32 White Street
Secondary School	Morgan Middle School	6th – 8th grade	Ms. Laura Chen, Principal	96 White Street
	Central High School	9th – 12th grade	Ms. Lisa Simmons, Principal	12 Glen Street
	Central Vocational High School	Job training	Mr. Martin Smith, Director	10 School Street
Post-Secondary Schools	Lincoln Community College	Two-year college	Ms. Alma Jones, Dean	2 King Street
	Martin Adult School	Continuing education for adults	Ms. Linda Brown, Dean	54 Main Street
	Glen State College	Four-year college	Dr. Sam Keating, President	45 University Drive

2 **WRITE.** Put the words in order. Make questions. Then write the answers.

1. Morgan Middle School/is/Where/?

   A: _Where is Morgan Middle School?_

   B: _It's on White Street._

2. Kennedy Elementary School/Is/Main Street/on/?

   A: _____

   B: _____

3. name/is/the/What/of the preschool?

   A: _____

   B: _____

4. is/Who/principal/the/of Central High School?

   A: _____

   B: _____

Write questions and answers from a chart. • Pronounce ordinal and cardinal numbers.

3 MATCH the questions with the answers.

___e___ 1. When is your son's birthday?

_____ 2. What is your daughter's name?

_____ 3. Where is the elementary school?

_____ 4. Where is the principal's office?

_____ 5. Who are they?

_____ 6. What grade is he in?

_____ 7. Is she in middle school?

_____ 8. Are your children in school?

a. Her name is Maria.

b. Yes, she is.

c. Yes, they are. They're in high school.

d. They are the custodians at this school.

e. It's December 14.

f. It's on 3rd Street.

g. He's in 8th grade.

h. It's in Room 24.

4 WRITE the questions. Use these question words: *What, Where,* and *When.*

1. *A:* _When is your daughter's birthday?_

   B: My daugher's birthdate is July 21.

2. *A:* _____

   B: My teacher's name is Linda Miller.

3. *A:* _____

   B: She is in the 4th grade.

4. *A:* _____

   B: The principal's office is in Room 70.

5. *A:* _____

   B: The high school is on Glen Street.

6. *A:* _____

   B: The students are in the classroom.

Pronunciation: *Ordinal and cardinal numbers*

TCD1, 13
SCD, 5

A LISTEN. Circle the words you hear.

| 1. | 30th | 30 | 3. | 13 | 30 | 5. | 70 | 70th |
| 2. | 13 | 30 | 4. | 3 | 3rd | 6. | 18th | 80th |

TCD1, 14
SCD 6

B LISTEN and repeat.

1. My daughter's birthday is March 30th.

2. My son is 13 years old.

3. There are 30 students in the class.

4. She is in the 3rd grade.

5. The principal's office is in Room 70.

6. The high school is on 80th Street.

LESSON 6: Apply Your Knowledge

1 **READ.** Look at the flier. Answer the questions below.

Washington Elementary School
Registration for New Students

Where: 35 Canal Street
When: August 12
Questions: Call the school at (513) 555-7720.

1. When is the registration? _It's on August 12._
2. Is the registration for new students? _____
3. What is the name of the school? _____
4. Is it a secondary school? _____
5. Where is the registration? _____
6. What is the school's phone number? _____

2 **WHAT ABOUT YOU?** Answer the questions below about your son or daughter or a child you know.

What grade is he or she in? _____

What is the name of the school? _____

Where is the school? _____

What is his or her teacher's name? _____

TCD1, 15
SCD, 7

3 **LISTEN** and read.

Mrs. Brown:	Good morning. Can I help you?
Charlotte:	Yes. My son is a new student.
Mrs. Brown:	What is his name?
Charlotte:	His name is Nicholas King.
Mrs. Brown:	Okay. What is your address?
Charlotte:	It's 12 Clinton Avenue.
Mrs. Brown:	What's your phone number?
Charlotte:	It's (513) 555-7617.
Mrs. Brown:	What grade is Nicholas in?
Charlotte:	He's in 1st grade.

TCD1, 16

LISTEN AGAIN and repeat. Then practice with a partner.

4 **PRACTICE THE CONVERSATION** with a partner.

1

Joe Wang
15 Elm Street
(513) 555-6202
9th grade

2

Debbie Dawson
25 Winter Street
(513) 555-3312
6th grade

3

Ben Wolf
37 Fort Street
(513) 555-2352
3rd grade

4

Maria Milton
92 School Street
(513) 555-8735
kindergarten

5 **WRITE.** Fill out the registration form for a person in Activity 4.

School Registration Form	
Name:	
Address:	
Phone:	
Grade:	

LESSON 7: Reading

1 **THINK ABOUT IT.** How many years of education are typical in your country?

2 **BEFORE YOU READ.** Look at the title of the article. What is the article about?

Reading Tip

Bar graphs are quick and easy ways to read information about numbers. In the bar graph below, we can quickly read the same information that is in the article. To read the bar graph, look at the numbers.

3 **READ** the article. Underline the money amounts.

It Pays to Stay in School

Some people leave school to get a job because they need money. However, people who stay in school usually make more money!

In 2006, people in the United States with some high school education earned an average salary of $18,734. People who finished high school earned an average of $27,915. People with a college or university degree earned an average of $51,206, and people with more than four years of college earned an average of $74,602. It pays to stay in school!

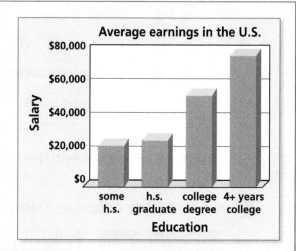

4 **CIRCLE** the correct answer.

1. The main idea of the article is that _____.

   a. you do not need college to make a lot of money

   b. people with more education make more money

2. The article says that sometimes people leave school _____.

   a. to get a job

   b. because they are bored

3. People with a college degree make _____ than people with a high school education.

   a. more

   b. less

5 **MATCH** the education and the average salary in the U.S.

_b_ 1. a college degree   a. $74,602

____ 2. some high school   b. $51,206

____ 3. more than four years of college c. $18,734

____ 4. a high school diploma   d. $27,915

Writing

1 EDIT. Underline the capital letters. Circle the periods.

> ### All About Me
>
> <u>M</u>y name is Andrea Lee. I am 30 years old. I am Taiwanese. I am short and thin. I have straight black hair and brown eyes. I am married. My husband's name is Tony. We have two daughters. Our older daughter is seven years old. Our younger daughter is two years old. I am a student at Weston Community College. I study English. My teacher's name is Jeff Donato.

2 WRITE. Answer the questions.

1. What is your name? _____

2. How old are you? _____

3. What is your nationality? _____

4. What do you look like? _____

5. Who is in your family? _____

6. What is the name of your school? _____

7. What do you study at school? _____

8. What is your teacher's name? _____

> **Writing Tip**
>
> All sentences begin with a **capital letter.** Also use capital letters for countries, days of the week, and names.
>
> All sentences end with a **period** (.), a **question mark** (?), or an **exclamation point** (!).

3 WRITE. Copy your answers from Activity 2 to write a paragraph about you. Use capital letters and periods.

All About Me

_____

_____

_____

_____

_____

_____

Career Connection

I'm going to be late today. Could you pick up a catalog at the college for me? Thanks!

My husband got a new job, so we're going to move next month.

I will begin looking for a new manager immediately. I'll interview people in two weeks.

We'll miss Lena!

Maybe I could be the new manager! I need a better salary.

You should apply for the job, Oscar!

2 **TALK.** With a partner, and answer the questions.

1. Where does Oscar work?

2. Why is Lena going to move?

3. When is Lena going to move?

4. Why does Oscar want to apply for the manager's job?

3 **WHAT ABOUT YOU?** Oscar wants a new job so he can have a better salary. Do you want a new job? Why?

Check Your Progress!

Skill	Circle the answers.		Is it correct?
A. Make present tense statements with *be*.	1. She **is**/**are** my daughter. 2. They **aren't**/**isn't** married. 3. I **am**/**is** single. 4. You **is**/**are** a good student.		☐ ☐ ☐ ☐
		Number Correct	0 1 2 3 4
B. Make present tense questions with *be*.	5. **Is you**/**Are you** a student? 6. **Is he**/**He is** a teacher? 7. **Who is**/**Where is** the school? 8. **Where are** / **Where is** the teachers?		☐ ☐ ☐ ☐
		Number Correct	0 1 2 3 4
C. Describe family members.	9. My granddaughter **is**/**has** twelve years old. 10. My grandmother **is**/**has** short black hair. 11. My son has hair on his chin. He has a **beard**/**mustache**. 12. My **son-in-law**/**daughter-in-law** is pregnant.		☐ ☐ ☐ ☐
		Number Correct	0 1 2 3 4
D. Talk about education in the United States.	13. 10th grade is in **elementary**/**secondary** school. 14. My daughter is in middle school she is in the **5th**/**1st** grade. 15. I am 42 years old. I go to **secondary school**/**adult school**. 16. My daughter is three years old. She goes to **elementary school**/**pre-school**.		☐ ☐ ☐ ☐
		Number Correct	0 1 2 3 4

COUNT the number of correct answers above. Fill in the circles.

Chart Your Success					
Skill	Needs More Practice	Needs More Practice	Okay	Very Good	Excellent!
A. Make present tense statements with *be*.	⓪	①	②	③	④
B. Make present tense questions with *be*.	⓪	①	②	③	④
C. Describe family members.	⓪	①	②	③	④
D. Talk about education in the United States.	⓪	①	②	③	④

LESSON 1: Grammar and Vocabulary

**TCD1, 18
SCD, 8**

1 GRAMMAR PICTURE DICTIONARY. Listen and repeat.

1 She is withdrawing cash from the **ATM**.

2 He is making a **deposit**.

3 They are opening a **bank account**.

4 She is **checking out** a book.

5 They are applying for **library cards**.

6 He is returning a book. It's **overdue**, and he is paying a **late fee**.

7 They are filling out a **change of address form**.

8 He is mailing a **package**.

9 She is waiting **in line**.

2 NOTICE THE GRAMMAR. Look at Activity 1. Underline the *be* verbs. Circle the verbs that end with *-ing*.

Present Continuous Statements

We use the present continuous to talk about actions happening right now.

Affirmative			Negative		
Subject	*be*	**Verb + *ing***	**Subject**	*be + not*	**Verb + *ing***
I	am		I	'm not	
You	are		You	aren't	
He / She	is	standing. walking. working.	He / She	isn't	sitting. running. sleeping.
We / You / They	are		We / You / They	aren't	

Spelling rules:

1. Add *-ing* to most verbs: **study – studying** **mail – mailing** **play – playing**
2. Words with *consonant + -e*, drop *-e* and add *-ing*: **take – taking** **use – using**
3. Words with *vowel + one consonant*, double the consonant and add *–ing*:
   run – running **stop – stopping**

> Never double the consonants *w, x,* or *y.*
>
> **Example:**
>
> *snow = snowing*

---

3 CIRCLE the correct answer.

1. Julia **is applying** / applying for a library card.
2. Ken **is** / **are** waiting in line at the bank.
3. **He's isn't** / **He's not** opening a checking account.
4. John **are checking** / **is checking** out a book.
5. I am **write** / **writing** a check to buy stamps.
6. They're **mail** / **mailing** a package at the post office.

4 WRITE the verb in the present continuous tense.

1. Ruth and Tony _____*are not returning*_____ (not return) a book.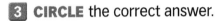
2. Mohammed _____ (run) in the park.
3. I _____ (not withdraw) cash.
4. Vicky _____ (mail) a letter at the post office.
5. Ken _____ (wait) in line.
6. You _____ (not make) a deposit.

LESSON 2: Grammar Practice Plus

Present Continuous Questions

Yes/No Questions

Be	Subject	Verb + ing
Am	I	
Are	you	
Is	he / she	learning? waiting? working?
Are	we / you / they	

Answers

	Subject	Verb
Yes,	I	am.
	you	are.
	he / she	is.
	we / you / they	are.

	Subject	Verb + not
No,	I	'm not.
	you	aren't.
	he / she	isn't.
	we / you / they	aren't.

Information Questions

Question Word	be	Subject	Verb + ing
What	are	you	doing?
Where	is	he	going?
Why	is	the bank	closing?

Answers

I'm making a deposit.
To the library.
Because it is 5:00.

---

1 WRITE. Complete the sentences. Then match the questions with the answers.

___c__ 1. Why _____is he paying_____ (he/pay) a late fee?   **a.** Yes, I am.

_____ 2. _____ (you/buy) stamps?   **b.** No, they aren't.

_____ 3. _____ (they/make) a deposit?   **c.** Because his book is overdue.

_____ 4. What _____ (you/do)?   **d.** At the library.

_____ 5. Where _____ (she/study)?   **e.** We're filling out forms.

2 WHAT ABOUT YOU? Look around your classroom. Answer the questions.

1. What is the teacher doing? _____

2. Is the teacher speaking? _____

3. What are the students doing? _____

4. Are the students listening to the teacher? _____

3 **TALK** about the picture.

The people are at a mall.

4 **LISTEN.** Write the correct number next to the name.

TCD1, 19

__4__ Tim   _____ Li Ping and Chen   _____ Sara and Todd

_____ Joe   _____ Sharon   _____ Bob

5 **CHECK** ☑ *true* or *false*.

1. Bob is applying for a library card.   ☐ true ☐ false

2. Sarah and Todd are waiting in line for the ATM.   ☐ true ☐ false

3. Sharon is opening a checking account.   ☐ true ☐ false

4. Tim is shopping for pants.   ☐ true ☐ false

5. Joe is mailing a letter.   ☐ true ☐ false

6 **TALK** with a partner. Point to people in the picture. Ask and answer questions.

Is she talking to her friend?

Yes, she is. She is talking to her friend and walking.

LESSON 3: Listening and Conversation

1 **CHECK.** Look at the pictures. What do you think is happening? Check ☑ your guesses.

Henry

Dr. Richards' Office

1. Henry is ...   ☐ at home.   ☐ at work.

2. Henry is ...   ☐ making a phone call.   ☐ sending an email.

3. Dr. Richards is...   ☐ in his office.   ☐ in the cafeteria.

4. Dr. Richards is...   ☐ talking to a patient.   ☐ eating lunch.

TCD1, 20

2 **LISTEN.** Match the people with the activities.

___d___ 1. Dr. Richards is . . .   **a.** teaching English class.

_____ 2. Ms. Bell is . . .   **b.** mailing a package at the post office.

_____ 3. Jennifer is . . .   **c.** talking to a patient.

_____ 4. Dr. Bloom is . . .   **d.** having lunch in the cafeteria.

_____ 5. Antonio is . . .   **e.** buying a new coat.

TCD1, 21

3 **LISTEN** to the question. Then listen to the conversation. Fill in the correct answer.

1. Ⓐ   Ⓑ   Ⓒ

2. Ⓐ   Ⓑ   Ⓒ

3. Ⓐ   Ⓑ   Ⓒ

4. Ⓐ   Ⓑ   Ⓒ

5. Ⓐ   Ⓑ   Ⓒ

6. Ⓐ   Ⓑ   Ⓒ

TCD1, 22
SCD, 9

4 **LISTEN** and read.

> A: Hello?
>
> B: Hi, this is Linh. May I speak to Sue?
>
> A: I'm, sorry. She's not here right now. She's at the mall. She's buying a birthday present.
>
> B: Okay, I'll call back later. Bye.
>
> A: Good-bye.

LISTEN AGAIN and repeat. Then practice with a partner.

TCD1, 23

5 **PRACTICE THE CONVERSATION** with a partner. Use your name for speaker B.

1 Steve/at the airport/
pick up his friend

2 Mrs. Brown/in her classroom/
teach math

3 Jerry/at the library/return a book

4 Linda/at a restaurant/have lunch

5 Mr. Lewis/at the post office/
mail a package

6 Yolanda/at the bank/
make a deposit

6 **WHAT ABOUT YOU?** Where are your friends and family members right now? What are they doing? Write one or two sentences.

Jose is in his office working.

_____

_____

7 **TALK** with a partner. Use the information in the Activity 4. Practice a phone conversation.

LESSON 4: Grammar and Vocabulary

TCD1, 24
SCD, 10

1 GRAMMAR PICTURE DICTIONARY. Listen and repeat.

1
A: Can I use this **coupon**?
B: I'm sorry, but you can't. Our store doesn't accept coupons.

2
A: Could I have a **receipt**, please?
B: Sure. No problem.

3
A: Could I please have **change** for a dollar?
B: Sure. Here are four quarters.

4
A: Could you tell me the **price**?
B: It's $10.00 plus **sales tax**.

5
A: May I **return** these shoes? They're too big.
B: Yes, of course.

6
A: May I **exchange** this necklace for a different one?
B: Sure. May I see your receipt?

7
A: Would you like a paper bag or a **plastic** bag?
B: Paper, please.

8
A: May I help you?
B: Yes, I'm looking for the shoe **department**.

9
A: Could I pay with a **credit card**?
B: Sorry, we only accept **cash**.

2 NOTICE THE GRAMMAR. Look at Activity 1. Circle *could*, *can*, *may* and *would like* in the questions.

Polite Requests and Offers

We use the modals *can*, *could*, *may*, and *would* to make polite requests and offers. *Could*, *may*, and *might* are more polite than *can*.

Requests

Modal	Subject	Verb	
Can Could Would	you	help	me?
Can Could May	I	have	a box?

Answers

Affirmative	Negative
Sure.	I'm sorry, I'm busy.
Of course. Yes, you can.	I'm sorry, we don't have boxes.

Offers

Modal	Subject	Verb	
Can Could May	I	help	you?

Answers

Affirmative	Negative
Yes, please.	No, thank you.

---

3 **CIRCLE** the correct word. Then match the question to the answer.

1. **Could** / **Would** I exchange this coat?

2. Can I **have** / **has** a plastic bag?

3. **May** / **Could** you tell me the price?

4. **Can** / **Would** I pay with a credit card?

5. **Would** / **Can** I help you?

a. _____ Of course. Here's one.

b. _____ Sorry. We only accept cash.

c. ___1___ I'm sorry. You need a receipt.

d. _____ Sure. It's $4.99.

e. _____ Yes, please. I want to buy this hat.

---

4 **WRITE.** Put the words in the correct order. Then write polite answers.

1. use / Could / pencil / I / your

   Could I use your pencil ? _Sure. Here it is._

2. smoke / I / Can / class / in

   _____ ? _____

3. work / I / you / May / with

   _____ ? _____

4. you / the / Could / open / door

   _____ ? _____

LESSON 5: Grammar Practice Plus

1 WRITE. Complete the questions. Use the words in the box.

exchange	refund	store credit

1

Clerk: Your _____ is $14.57.
Customer: Thanks.

2

Customer: Could I _____ this red shirt for a green one?
Clerk: Of course.

3

Customer: Could I have a refund?
Clerk: I'm sorry. We can't give you a refund. We can only give you a _____.

 LISTEN AND REPEAT. Are your answers correct?

TCD1, 25

2 CHECK ☑ the correct answer.

1. *Customer:* Can I return this jacket? I don't have a receipt.
   Salesclerk: ☐ Yes, please.
   ☐ I'm sorry. You can't.

2. *Customer:* Could I get a store credit?
   Salesclerk: ☐ Sure.
   ☐ No, they aren't.

3. *Customer:* I have a receipt for this shirt. Can I get a refund?
   Salesclerk: ☐ Yes, you can.
   ☐ No, thank you.

4. *Customer:* May I exchange these shoes for a different size?
   Salesclerk: ☐ Yes, of course.
   ☐ I'm sorry. I can't.

5. *Customer:* Could you help me?
   Salesclerk: ☐ No, thank you.
   ☐ I'm sorry, I'm helping another customer.

TALK. Practice the conversations with a partner.

3 **WRITE** the question. Use *can*, *could*, or *may*.

1. You want to exchange a blue coat for a black coat.

   Could I exchange this blue coat for a black one _____ ?

2. You want to return a shirt.

   _____ ?

3. You want a refund.

   _____ ?

4. You want to return a camera.

   _____ ?

Pronunciation: *Could you (couldya)*

TCD1, 26
SCD, 11

A **LISTEN** and repeat.

1. Could you help me?

2. Could you give me a refund, please?

3. Could you give me a store credit?

4. Could you tell me the price?

TCD1, 27
SCD 12

B **LISTEN** to the sentences. Circle the words you hear.

1. Could **you** / she   4. Could **you** / I

2. Could **you** / I   5. Could **you** / she

3. Could **you** / he

---

4 **WRITE** three requests to ask a partner.

My requests	Partner's answers
1. Could you tell me the time?	Sure. It's 10:15.
2.	
3.	

TALK. Ask the questions. Write your partner's answers.

LESSON 6: Apply Your Knowledge

1 **READ** the information below. Circle the things you have checked out from a library.

Bedford Public Library Rules and Late Fee Information			
	Check out time	Renew?	Late fee
Books	2 weeks	yes – twice (2 times)	25¢ / day
CDs (music)	1 week	yes – once (1 time)	$1.00 / day
DVDs (movie)	1 week	no	$2.00 / day
Video tapes (movie)	2 weeks	yes – once (1 time)	$1.00 / day

TCD1, 28

2 **LISTEN** to the dialogues. Answer the questions. Circle *yes* or *no*.

Questions	Librarian's answers	
1. Can I check out a DVD?	yes	no
2. Could I renew this book?	yes	no
3. Could I check out this magazine?	yes	no
4. Can I check out this book?	yes	no
5. May I renew this CD?	yes	no

Math: Calculate Late Fees

READ the chart in Activity 1. What are the late fees for the people below?

Example: John is returning three overdue books at the library. The books are five days overdue. How much is the late fee?

Information: For one book, the late fee is $.25 per day.
Step one: For one book, multiply number of days times late fee: 5 X $ .25 = $1.25.
Step two: For three books, multiply 3 times the late fee for one book: 3 X $1.25 = $3.75.
Answer: The late fee is $3.75.

1. Mr. Brown is returning two overdue books and an overdue DVD. The books and the DVD are five days late. How much is the late fee? _____

2. Jane is returning overdue books and CDs. She has two CDs and five books. The books and CDs are three days late. How much is the late fee? _____

3. Andrea has two overdue videotapes and three overdue CDs. They are all six days late. How much is the late fee? _____

3 **LISTEN** and read.

TCD1, 29
SCD, 13

Man:	Hi. Can I renew a book?
Librarian:	Sure. You can renew it once.
Man:	Could I also check out this map?
Librarian:	No, I'm sorry. You can't check out maps. Would you like anything else?
Man:	No, that's all. Thank you.

4 **PRACTICE THE CONVERSATION** from Activity 3 with a partner.

1

check out / DVD / check it out until August 20 / check out this dictionary

2

renew / CD / renew it once / check out this magazine

3

renew / book / renew it twice / renew these DVDs

4

check out / videotape / check it out until March 4 / check out this newspaper

 5 **WHAT ABOUT YOU?** Do you go to the library? Do you sometimes have questions? Write four requests.

1. Could _____?

2. Can _____?

3. May _____?

4. Could _____?

Could you help me find books about cooking?

May I check out this DVD?

LESSON 7: Reading

1 THINK ABOUT IT. Do you send and receive email? Do you send and receive letters? Do you send and receive text messages?

Reading Tip

Before you read an email, quickly **scan** the message. Look for (1) the day or date of the message, (2) who the message is from, and (3) who the message is to.

2 BEFORE YOU READ. Scan the email. Circle the date, who the message is to, and who the message is from.

3 READ. <u>Underline</u> the activities (present continuous verbs) in the email.

FROM: Martha Thomas
TO: Sam Johnson
SENT: April 4, 3:30 PM
SUBJECT: Hi

Hi Sam,

How are you? I'm <u>thinking</u> about you! What are you doing? Of course, I know the answer. You're reading this message on your computer!

I am relaxing in my bedroom and writing you this note. My family isn't relaxing. My mother is cleaning the house. My father is at the mall. He is exchanging some clothes. My sister is at the bank. She's opening an account. They are all very busy.

How are you? How is your new job? How is your new apartment? Could you send me some photos? Write me soon!

Martha

4 ANSWER the question. Circle the main idea of the email.

a. Martha is busy, and her family is busy, too.

b. Martha is relaxing, but her family is busy.

c. Martha and Sam are friends.

5 EDIT. Cross out the mistakes in the sentences. Write the correct words.

1. Martha's mother is cleaning the ~~car.~~ *house*

2. Martha is studying in her bedroom.

3. Her father is at work.

4. He is buying some things.

5. Martha's sister is closing a bank account.

6. Martha's sister is at the mall.

Writing

1 **EDIT** the email. Add periods, question marks, capital letters, and commas.

Check mail   Compose   Search mail   Search Web

(1) **Inbox**

Draft

(2) **Sent**

Bulk

Trash

G
dear george

how are you i'm using the computer at the library the library is a

busy place many people are reading   some students are taking a

computer class the teacher is helping the students   my friend is

here with me she is studying her English

lesson many people are looking for books

this is a nice library I like to come here

could you write to me soon

mary

2 **WRITE** a note to a friend. Write about your classmates or family members and the activities they are doing right now.

_____

_____

_____

_____

_____

3 **EDIT** your note for capital letters, question marks, commas, and periods.

1 READ AND LISTEN. Then practice with a partner.

TCD1, 30

1
Look, Oscar, the manager's job is on the board.

Really? That's great, Eric!

2
"Strong leadership skills. Computer skills necessary." Hmm.

3
How can I learn computer skills in two or three weeks?

Well, you can check out a book about computers from the library. Or you can take a class at night school.

4
Good idea, Eric! I'll look at the class schedule tonight.

I'm taking a cooking class right now. You can learn a lot in a few weeks.

2 CHECK ☑ *yes* or *no*.

1. The manager's job is posted on the job board.	☐ yes	☐ no
2. Oscar has computer skills.	☐ yes	☐ no
3. The library has books about computers.	☐ yes	☐ no
4. Eric is taking a cooking class now.	☐ yes	☐ no

3 WHAT ABOUT YOU? Can you use a computer? Can you cook? What new skills do you want to learn?

Check Your Progress!

Skill	Circle the answers.	Is it correct?				
A. Make present continuous statements.	1. Bob **is makes** / **is making** a deposit. 2. Maria **is checking out** / **checking out** a book. 3. David and Linda **is returning** / **are returning** a book. 4. He **isn't waiting** / **doesn't waiting** in line.	☐ ☐ ☐ ☐				
	Number Correct	0	1	2	3	4

Skill	Circle the answers.	Is it correct?				
B. Make present continuous questions.	5. **What** / **Where** are they going? To the library. 6. **Why** / **What** is he paying a late fee? Because the book is overdue. 7. Where **is** / **are** Mike and Linda studying? At Linda's house. 8. Are Sue and Lee mailing a package? **No, they aren't.** / **Yes, she is**.	☐ ☐ ☐ ☐				
	Number Correct	0	1	2	3	4

Skill	Circle the answers.	Is it correct?				
C. Make polite requests at the store.	9. **Would** / **Could** I exchange this shirt? 10. **Would** / **Why** you like a plastic or paper bag? 11. **May** / **Would** I return these shoes. 12. **Would** / **Can** I use this coupon?	☐ ☐ ☐ ☐				
	Number Correct	0	1	2	3	4

Skill	Circle the answers.	Is it correct?				
D. Use the library.	13. How much is the late fee? **It's $1.50** / **It's two days**. 14. I'm paying a late fee because the DVD is **renew** / **overdue**. 15. I'm sorry you can't **overdue** / **check out** newspapers. 16. I want the book for one more week. May I **renew** / **late fee** it?	☐ ☐ ☐ ☐				
	Number Correct	0	1	2	3	4

COUNT the number of correct answers above. Fill in the circles.

Chart Your Success					
Skill	Needs Practice	Needs Practice	Okay	Very Good	Excellent!
A. Make present continuous statements.	⓪	①	②	③	④
B. Make present continuous questions.	⓪	①	②	③	④
C. Make polite requests at the store.	⓪	①	②	③	④
D. Use the library.	⓪	①	②	③	④

LESSON 1: Grammar and Vocabulary

1 **GRAMMAR PICTURE DICTIONARY.** Listen and repeat.

TCD1, 31
SCD, 14

1
Every morning, Gloria and Leon Cruz **get** their children **ready** for school.

2
Leon **takes** the children to school in the morning. He **picks up** the children in the afternoon.

3
In the morning, Gloria and Leon **attend** English classes.

4
Gloria and Leon are sometimes very tired, but they don't **miss** class.

5
They **both** have **part-time jobs** in the afternoon.

6
After school, the children help their parents with the **chores**.

7
The children **set the table** and Gloria and Leon **prepare dinner**.

8
They **do homework** or **relax** after dinner.

9
They **do the housework** in the evening.

2 **NOTICE THE GRAMMAR.** Look at Activity 1. <u>Underline</u> the verbs.

Simple Present Tense

We use simple present to talk about activities that we do again and again.

Affirmative

Subject	Verb	
I You	relax	
He She	relaxes	in the morning. on Monday.
We You They	relax	

Negative

Subject	*do + not*	Verb	
I You	don't		
He She	doesn't	relax	in the morning. on Monday.
We You They	don't		

Spelling rules for simple present:

1. Add *-s* to the base form of a verb (for *He, She, It*): start → start**s**,   walk → walk**s**
2. For verbs ending in consonant + *-y*, change *-y* to *-i* and add *-es*: study → stud**ies**, carry → carr**ies**
3. For verbs ending in vowel + *-y*, add *-s*: buy → buy**s**,   pay → pay**s**
4. For verbs ending in *-s*, *-z*, *-ch*, *-sh*, and *-x*, add *-es*: relax → relax**es**, watch → watch**es**

---

3 **WRITE.** Complete the sentences. Use the present tense.

1. Ana and Tom ___*don't attend*___ (not attend) school on Saturday.

2. She _____ (study) English in the evening.

3. I _____ (not do) homework on Saturday.

4. Their father _____ (prepare) breakfast in the morning.

5. They _____ (relax) in the evening.

6. He _____ (not go) to work in the afternoon.

4 **WHAT ABOUT YOU?** Complete the sentences. Write affirmative or negative sentences.

1. I _____ (attend) class on Monday.

2. I _____ (arrive) at school on time.

3. I _____ (watch) TV in the morning.

4. I _____ (have) a part-time job.

5. I _____ (do) housework on the weekend.

TALK. Read your sentences to a partner.

LESSON 2: Grammar Practice Plus

1 **LISTEN AND REPEAT.** Number the activities.

Wednesday Routines

Saturday Routines

2 **WRITE.** Complete the sentences. Use words from the box. Use the present tense.

1. On Wednesdays, *Pete does the laundry* _____.

2. Susan _____.

3. Andy and Becky _____.

4. On Saturdays, Pete _____.

5. Susan _____.

6. Andy _____.

7. Becky and her friend _____.

watch videos
send messages and do homework
shop for food
sleep late
do the laundry
wash the car
go to the gym

He sleeps late on Saturday.

Andy?

Yes!

3 **GAME.** Work with a partner. Look at the pictures on page 40. Take turns.

Student A: Make a statement about a person's routine on Wednesday or Saturday.

Student B: Say the person's name.

4 **WHAT ABOUT YOU?** Check ☑ your activities for Wednesday and Saturday. Add two more activities and check ☑ the days you do them.

		Wednesday	Saturday
1.	go to work		
2.	attend class		
3.	do laundry		
4.	do homework		
5.	relax		
6.	prepare dinner		
7.	sleep late		
8.	help my children with homework		
9.			
10.			

5 **TALK** to three classmates about their routines.

Name	Kim			
What do you do on Wednesdays?	go to work attend class			
What do you do on Saturdays?	sleep late exercise			

6 **WRITE** sentences about your classmates' routines.

Example: _Kim goes to work on Wednesdays. She exercises on Saturdays._

1. _____

2. _____

3. _____

LESSON 3: Listening and Conversation

Pronunciation: Final *s* sounds: *s*, *z*, and *iz*

A LISTEN AND REPEAT. Circle the sound for the final *s*.

TCD1, 33
SCD, 15

1. She takes the children to school. (s) z iz
2. He helps with the housework. s z iz
3. She washes the car every week. s z iz
4. He cooks dinner. s z iz
5. He does homework in the evening. s z iz

B TALK with a partner. Say the words below. Write the words in the chart.

asks	brushes	cleans	exercises
goes	helps	runs	speaks
studies	talks	teaches	watches

s	z	iz
asks		

1 LISTEN to the question. Then listen to the phone conversation. Fill in the correct answer.

TCD1, 34

1. (A) (B) (C)   3. (A) (B) (C)   5. (A) (B) (C)
2. (A) (B) (C)   4. (A) (B) (C)   6. (A) (B) (C)

2 LISTEN. Write the appointment days and times.

TCD1, 35

SPENCER DENTAL OFFICE

Day _____
Time _____

Linn's BEAUTY SHOP

Day _____
Time _____

3 **LISTEN** and read.

> *A:* Hi. I'd like an appointment for a haircut this week.
>
> *B:* How about Wednesday afternoon?
>
> *A:* Oh, I'm sorry. I go to the gym on Wednesday afternoons.
>
> *B:* Can you come on Friday morning?
>
> *A:* Sure, that's fine.

LISTEN AGAIN and repeat. Then practice with a partner.

4 **PRACTICE THE CONVERSATION** with a partner.

1

for a carpet cleaning / help in my child's class

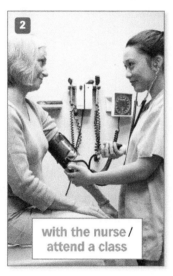

2

with the nurse / attend a class

3

for some car repairs / work

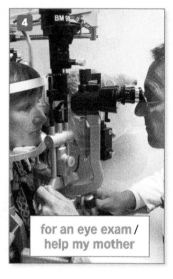

4

for an eye exam / help my mother

5 **WHAT ABOUT YOU?** Complete the calendar with your usual morning and afternoon activities.

	Monday	Tuesday	Wednesday	Thursday	Friday	Saturday
Morning						
Afternoon						

TALK with a partner. Make appointments. Use your schedule. Follow the example in Activity 3.

LESSON 4: Grammar and Vocabulary

TCD1, 38
SCD, 17

1 GRAMMAR PICTURE DICTIONARY. Listen and repeat.

1 At **break time**, she sometimes makes calls on her cell phone.

2 He usually buys a **snack**.

3 They always have **conversations** in English.

4 He sometimes takes a **short nap**.

5 They usually use the **restroom**.

6 He sometimes sends **text messages** to his friends.

7 They usually listen to **music**.

8 She sometimes **checks** her **email**.

9 They never **return** to class **late** after break time.

2 NOTICE THE GRAMMAR. Look at Activity 1. Underline the verbs. Circle the words that explain how often: *always, usually, sometimes, never*.

Adverbs of Frequency

Adverbs of frequency usually come after the subject and before the verb.

Subject	Adverb of Frequency	Verb	
I You	always (100%)		in English.
He She	usually sometimes	speak(s)	in Spanish. in Chinese.
We You They	rarely never (0%)		in French.

Expressions of Frequency

Expressions of frequency usually come at the end of a sentence.

Subject	Verb	Expression of Frequency
I You	study	every day. every weekend.
He She	takes a test	every month. every year.
We You They	check email	once a day. twice a day. three times a day.

3 WRITE. Put the words in order to make sentences.

1. buy / at / snack / a / once a week / I / break time / .

   I buy a snack at break time once a week.

2. usually / makes / He / on / calls / phone / cell / his / .

   _____

3. never / email / break time / They / check / at / .

   _____

4. break time / She / rest room / uses / usually / the / at / .

   _____

5. every day / conversations / have / They / in English / .

   _____

4 WHAT ABOUT YOU? Write about your routine. Use *always, usually, sometimes, rarely, never.*

1 I _____ have a snack at break time.

2. I _____ talk to my teacher after class.

3. I _____ practice English at break time.

4. I _____ come to class late.

5. I _____ study at night.

6. I _____ think in English.

TALK. Read your sentences to a partner.

LESSON 5: Grammar Practice Plus

1 **WRITE.** Look at the classroom activities for one week. Complete the sentences under the pictures. Use the words in the box.

once a week	twice a week	three times a week	every day

Classroom Activities				
Monday	**Tuesday**	**Wednesday**	**Thursday**	**Friday**
• 8:30: Class begins	• 8:30: Class begins	• 8:30: Class begins	• 8:30: Class begins	• 8:30: Class begins
• Practice with partners	• Practice with partners	• Practice with partners	• Practice with partners	• Practice with partners
• Use flash cards	• Use flash cards	• Listening practice	• Use flash cards	• Test
• Listening practice	• Write paragraphs	• Dictionary work	• Write paragraphs	

1 They look up words in the dictionary _____.

2 They practice with partners _____.

3 They write paragraphs _____.

4 They come to class on time _____.

5 They have a test _____.

6 They use flash cards _____.

2 **LISTEN** and repeat. Are your answers correct?

3 **WHAT ABOUT YOU?** Talk in a group. How do you learn English in class? How do you learn English outside of class? Write activities in the chart.

Ways we learn English in class	Ways we learn English outside of class
practice with a partner	*watch TV in English*

4 **WRITE** sentences. How do you learn English?

Example: *I never watch TV in English.* **OR** *I watch TV in English every day.*

1. listen to music in English _____

2. send text messages in English _____

3. send email in English _____

4. talk on the phone in English _____

5. speak English at work _____

6. watch TV in English _____

7. (other) _____

Math: Complete a graph

READ the information. Complete the graph.

The students at Spencer School practice English in many different ways. The school asked the students, "How do you use English outside of class?" 200 students answered. 175 students reported they watch TV in English. 100 students speak English at work. 125 students sometimes listen to music in English and 75 students sometimes talk on the phone in English. 50 students read the newspaper in English, but only 25 send email messages in English.

DRAW bars on the graph to show how many students practice English in each way.

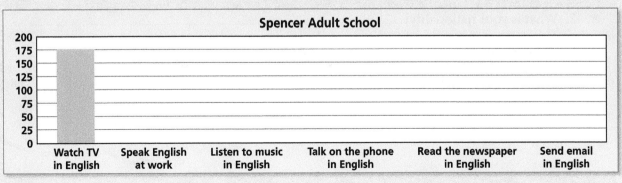

LESSON 6: Apply Your Knowledge

TCD1, 40

1 **LISTEN** to the conversation. Circle the correct answers.

1. Who is the new student?
   A. Antonio   B. Samuel

2. What is the new student's last name?
   A. Mohammed   B. Mahamud

3. What is his nationality?
   A. Somali   B. Sudanese

4. What street does he live on?
   A. Elm Avenue   B. Oak Street

5. How many dependents does he have?
   A. five   B. fifteen

TCD1, 41

LISTEN AGAIN. Complete the form for the new student.

> Your children (younger than 18) are your **dependents**. You give them food and a place to live. Your parents can be your dependents, too.

Please answer these questions.
1. What is your nationality?
2. What is your address?
3. What is your first and last name?
4. How many dependents do you have?

2 **WHAT ABOUT YOU?** Talk with a partner. Ask and answer the questions.

1. Could you spell your name, please? _____

2. What is your nationality? _____

3. What language do you usually speak at home? _____

TALK. Introduce your partner to the class.

> This is Marta Lopez. She speaks Spanish and English at home. Her nationality is Cuban.

Share nationality, language, and personal information. • Read a schedule.

3 **LISTEN** and read.

A: Hi. I'm Leon. I'm the class helper today. Could I tell you about our conversation class?

B: Sure. Thanks.

A: Class starts at 9:00 A.M. We take a break from 10:20 to 10:40. Class ends at 11:30.

B: Okay. How often do you have tests?

A: We have tests once a week.

B: Thanks for the information!

LISTEN AGAIN and repeat. Then practice with a partner.

4 **PRACTICE THE CONVERSATION** with a partner. Use your own name for the class helper.

	1 Writing class	**2** Computer class	**3** Citizenship class
Class starts	8:30 A.M.	1:00 P.M.	7:00 P.M.
Break time	10:00 to 10:15 A.M.	2:00 to 2:15 P.M.	7:45 to 7:55 P.M.
Class ends	11:45 A.M.	3:30 P.M.	9:00 P.M.
Test schedule	twice a month	once a month	once a week

5 **WHAT ABOUT YOU?** Answer the questions about your class.

1. What time does your class start? _____

2. Does your class take a break? What time? _____

3. What time does your class end? _____

4. How often do you have tests? _____

5. How often do you write a paragraph? _____

TALK with a partner about your class. Follow the conversation in Activity 3.

LESSON 7: Reading

1 THINK ABOUT IT. What day of the week is busy for you? What day is fun?

Reading Tip

Look for **time expressions** (*in the morning, at 3:00, after that*) as you read. Time expressions tell the order of activities.

2 BEFORE YOU READ. Look at the titles. What do you think the stories are about?

3 READ. Circle the time expressions as you read. Who are you more similar to, Carol or David?

A Busy Day

Wednesday is a busy day for me. In the morning, I take my children to school, and then I attend my English class from 8:30 to 11:30. In the afternoon, I usually go grocery shopping or clean the house. Sometimes I also do laundry. At 3:00, I pick up my children from school. Then I help them with their homework. At 5:00, I cook dinner for my husband and two children. We always eat dinner at 6:00. After dinner, I read stories to my children and prepare their lunches for the next day. I usually go to bed at 9:30, but sometimes I'm very tired, and I fall asleep in front of the TV!

Carol Jonas

A Fun Day

Sunday is usually a fun day for me. I sleep late, I have a nice breakfast, and then I go for a walk. After that, I call my parents, sisters, brothers, aunts, and uncles. They live in many different cities. My cell phone calls are free on Sunday! I always talk on the phone for a long time. In the afternoon, I sometimes go to a movie or go shopping with my friends. In the evening, I usually watch TV, but sometimes I read a book. I work very hard on weekdays, but I never work on Sundays. I relax and have fun!

David Paine

4 READ the statements. Circle *True* or *False*.

1. On Wednesday, Carol attends class in the afternoon.   **True**   **False**

2. She usually does housework in the afternoon.   **True**   **False**

3. She and her family always eat dinner at 5:00.   **True**   **False**

4. David usually sleeps late on Sunday.   **True**   **False**

5. He does housework in the afternoon.   **True**   **False**

6. He relaxes on Sunday.   **True**   **False**

Writing

1 **WRITE.** Choose a day of the week. Think about your usual routine for that day. Answer the questions.

1. What is the day?

   _____

2. What do you do in the morning?

   _____

3. What do you do in the afternoon?

   _____

4. What do you do at night?

   _____

> ### Writing Tip
>
> The *title* is a name for a story or other writing. It tells the reader what the story is about. Use a capital letter for the first word in the title and for all important words.
>
> **Examples:**
> *A Usual Monday*
> *My Saturday Schedule*
> *A Day at School*

2 **WRITE** a paragraph about the day in Activity 1. Make a title for your story.

_____

I want to tell you about my usual routine on _____.

In the morning, I _____

_____.

In the afternoon, I _____.

At night, I _____

_____.

3 **EDIT** your writing.

☐ Does each sentence start with a capital letter?

☐ Does each sentence end with a period?

☐ Is there a title?

4 **WRITE** your paragraph again on a piece of paper.

1 READ AND LISTEN. Then practice with a partner.

TCD1, 44

2 TALK. When can Oscar take classes? Why can't Maggie work on Mondays and Wednesdays during the day?

3 WHAT ABOUT YOU? Do you have a job? What days do you work? What days do you go to class? Who makes your work schedule?

Check Your Progress!

Skill	Circle the correct words.	Is it correct?				
A. Make statements in simple present tense.	1. Gloria **relax** / **relaxes** on Sundays. 2. He **doesn't have** / **doesn't has** a job. 3. They **do** / **does** homework after dinner. 4. Martin **don't** / **doesn't** work on Saturdays	☐ ☐ ☐ ☐				
	Number Correct	0	1	2	3	4
B. Talk about frequency of routine activities.	5. He **never drinks** / **drinks never** coffee. 6. He **usually check** / **usually checks** his email at break time. 7. She works on Tuesdays and Thursdays. She works **once** / **twice** a week. 8. I take my son to soccer practice every Thursday. He has practice **once** / **twice** a week.	☐ ☐ ☐ ☐				
	Number Correct	0	1	2	3	4
C. Talk about things you do at school.	9. The students **have** / **make** a test every Friday. 10. We take a break from 10:00 **to** / **at** 10:15. 11. The students **practice with** / **practice for** partners. 12. The students check their spelling in their **dictionaries** / **math**.	☐ ☐ ☐ ☐				
	Number Correct	0	1	2	3	4
D. List ways to learn more English.	13. I come to class **at time** / **on time** every day. 14. I **always** / **rarely** miss class. 15. I **look up** / **look down** new words in the dictionary. 16. I listen to music **in English** / **for English**.	☐ ☐ ☐ ☐				
	Number Correct	0	1	2	3	4

COUNT the number of correct answers above. Fill in the circles.

Chart Your Success					
Skill	Needs Practice	Needs Practice	Okay	Very Good	Excellent!
A. Make statements in simple present tense.	⓪	①	②	③	④
B. Talk about frequency of routine activities.	⓪	①	②	③	④
C. Talk about things you do at school.	⓪	①	②	③	④
D. List ways to learn more English.	⓪	①	②	③	④

LESSON 1: Grammar and Vocabulary

TCD2, 2
SCD, 19

1 **GRAMMAR PICTURE DICTIONARY.** Listen and repeat.

1
A: Does she need a **driver's license**?
B: Yes, she does.

2
A: Does he have **work experience**?
B: Yes, he does.

3
A: Does he have a **high school diploma**?
B: Yes, he does.

4
A: Does the job **require computer skills**?
B: Yes, it does.

5
A: Does she **assist** with **patients**?
B: Yes, she does.

6
A: Does she earn a good **salary**?
B: No, she doesn't.

7
A: Does he have a **part-time job**?
B: No, he doesn't. He has a **full-time job**.

8
A: Do they work the **day shift**?
B: No they don't. They work the **night shift**.

9
A: Does his work **schedule include** weekends?
B: No, it doesn't.

2 **NOTICE THE GRAMMAR.** Look at Activity 1. Circle the verbs.

Simple Present Tense: *Yes/No* Questions and Answers

Questions				Answers					
Do	Subject	Verb			Subject	*do*		Subject	*do*
Do	I you				I you	do.		I you	don't.
Does	he she it	work?	Yes,		he she it	does.	No,	he she it	doesn't.
Do	we you they				we you they	do.		we you they	don't.

3 **MATCH** the questions to the answers.

__c__ 1. Does Bob have computer skills?

_____ 2. Do they earn a good salary?

_____ 3. Does Tomas have a full-time job?

_____ 4. Do they work the night shift?

_____ 5. Does Sara work on weekends?

_____ 6. Do the nurses assist the doctors?

a. No, she doesn't. She works Monday through Friday.

b. No, he doesn't. He has a part-time job.

c. Yes, he does. He has excellent skills.

d. No, they don't. Their pay is low.

e. Yes, they do. They help the doctors every day.

f. No, they don't. They work from 9:00 A.M. to 5:00 P.M.

4 **WHAT ABOUT YOU?** Write the words in the correct order to make questions and write your answers.

Question   **Answer**

1. have / you / Do / computer skills / ?

   Do you have computer skills?   _____

2. work / have / you / Do / experience / ?

   _____   _____

3. part-time / you / Do / job / a / have / ?

   _____   _____

4. have / you / Do / license / a / driver's / ?

   _____   _____

TALK. Ask and answer the questions with a partner.

LESSON 2: Grammar Practice Plus

1 **LISTEN** and number the people in the picture.

2 **MATCH** the positions to the responsibilities.

Positions	Responsibilities
1. __b__ cashier	**a.** fly airplanes
2. _____ manager	**b.** collect money and make change
3. _____ gardener	**c.** take care of plants
4. _____ pilot	**d.** inspect luggage
5. _____ flight attendant	**e.** supervise workers
6. _____ security agent	**f.** help passengers during flights

3 **TALK** with a partner. Ask and answer questions about the jobs above.

Does the cashier supervise the workers?

No, he doesn't. He collects money and makes change.

4 **WRITE** questions with *do* or *does*. Then write answers.

1. A: _Do flight attendants work on weekends?_

   B: Yes, they _____do_____ . Flight attendants often work on weekends.

2. A: _____

   B: No, they _____ . Pilots do not inspect luggage.

3. A: _____

   B: Yes, she _____ . The cashier collects money and makes change.

4. A: _____

   B: Yes, he _____ . The gardener takes care of plants.

5. A: _____

   B: No, they _____ . Pilots don't serve food to customers.

6. A: _____

   B: Yes, they _____ . Airport security agents inspect luggage.

5 **WRITE.** Complete the questions and answers. Use *do*, *does*, *is*, or *are*.

1. A: ___Do___ they work the day shift?   B: No, they ___don't___ .

2. A: _____ he a manager?   B: Yes, he _____ .

3. A: _____ he supervise the workers?   B: Yes, he _____ .

4. A: _____ you have computer skills?   B: Yes, I _____ .

5. A: _____ you students?   B: Yes, we _____ .

6. A: _____ she assist the manager?   B: Yes, she _____ .

7. A: _____ they cashiers?   B: No, they _____ .

8. A: _____ they work at a restaurant?   B: Yes, they _____ .

6 **TALK** with a partner. Ask and answer questions.

have a job	work on weekends
have computer skills	work the day shift
have work experience	have a driver's license
have a good work schedule	speak English at work

Do you have a driver's license?

No, I don't.

LESSON 3: Listening and Conversation

Pronunciation: Questions with *Does he* or *Does she*

TCD2, 4
SCD, 20

A LISTEN AND REPEAT.

1. Does he earn a good salary?   Does she earn a good salary?

2. Does he collect money?   Does she collect money?

3. Does he supervise workers?   Does she supervise workers?

4. Does he assist with patients?   Does she assist with patients?

5. Does he inspect luggage?   Does she inspect luggage?

6. Does he fly airplanes?   Does she fly airplanes?

TCD2, 5
SCD, 21

B LISTEN. Circle the letter of the correct answer.

1. a. Yes, he does.   b. Yes, she does.

2. a. Yes, he does.   b. Yes, she does.

3. a. No, he doesn't.   b. No, she doesn't.

4. a. No, he doesn't.   b. No, she doesn't.

5. a. Yes, he does.   b. Yes, she does.

6. a. No, he doesn't.   b. No, she doesn't.

TCD2, 6

1 LISTEN to the question. Then listen to the conversation. Fill in the correct answer.

1. Ⓐ Ⓑ Ⓒ   4. Ⓐ Ⓑ Ⓒ

2. Ⓐ Ⓑ Ⓒ   5. Ⓐ Ⓑ Ⓒ

3. Ⓐ Ⓑ Ⓒ   6. Ⓐ Ⓑ Ⓒ

TCD2, 7

2 LISTEN to the first part of a conversation. Then listen to three possible answers to finish the conversation. Fill in the correct answer.

1. Ⓐ Ⓑ Ⓒ   4. Ⓐ Ⓑ Ⓒ

2. Ⓐ Ⓑ Ⓒ   5. Ⓐ Ⓑ Ⓒ

3. Ⓐ Ⓑ Ⓒ   6. Ⓐ Ⓑ Ⓒ

TCD2, 8
SCD, 22

3 **LISTEN** and read.

A: What kind of job are you looking for?

B: I'm looking for a job as a car salesperson.

A: Do you have experience?

B: Yes, I do. I have two years' experience.

A: Do you want a full-time job or a part-time job?

B: I'm looking for a full-time job.

TCD2, 9

LISTEN AGAIN and repeat. Then practice with a partner.

4 **PRACTICE THE CONVERSATION** with a partner.

1

teachers' aide/
1 year/part-time

2

restaurant manager/
3 years'/full-time

3

administrative assistant/
1 year/part-time

4

bus driver/
1 year/part-time

5

security guard/
2 years'/full-time

6

flight attendent/
5 years'/full-time

5 **WHAT ABOUT YOU?** Talk with a partner. Ask and answer questions. Follow the conversation in Activity 3.

LESSON 4: Grammar and Vocabulary

1 GRAMMAR PICTURE DICTIONARY. Listen and repeat.

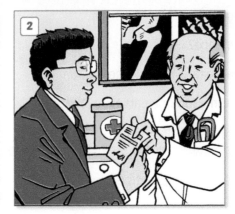

A: (What) **benefits** <u>does</u> the company <u>offer</u>?
B: It offers **sick leave benefits**, **health insurance**, and five **vacation days**.

A: What does the **union** do?
B: It helps workers get good pay and have **safe working conditions**.

Hours	
Regular Hours	40 at $11.00 per hr
Overtime Hours	6 at $15.75 per hr
Pay	
Total regular pay	
Total overtime pay	
Total Earned	
Deductions (taxes, health insurance)	
Total Pay for Week	

A: How much does the company pay for **overtime**?
B: It pays $15.75 an hour for overtime.

A: Where do the employees take breaks?
B: They take breaks in the **employee lounge**.

Morris Library Employment Application

Name:
Address:
Phone:
Email:
Birth.

A: How do I apply?
B: You fill out an **application** online.

2 NOTICE THE GRAMMAR. <u>Underline</u> *do* and *does* and the base form of the verbs in the sentences above. (Circle) the question words.

Use information questions. • Listen and discuss employee benefits.

Simple Present Tense: Information Questions

To ask for information, use: *who, what, where, when, why,* and *how.*

Information Questions				Answers	
Question Word	***do/does***	**Subject**	**Verb**		
Where	do	you	work?	I work at Spencer Hospital.	
When	do	you	work?	I work the night shift.	
What	does	it	cost?	It costs $20.	
Who	does	he/she	work with?	He/She works with Fred.	
Why	do	they	go home early?	Because they start work early.	
How	do	they	get to work?	They take the bus.	
How much	do	they	pay for overtime?	They pay $14.50 per hour.	

3 **WRITE** the question words.

1. *A:* _____Where_____ does he work?

   B: He works **at Atlas Bank**.

2. *A:* _____ does Jim supervise?

   B: Jim supervises **Sarah and Bob**.

3. *A:* _____ do they take their break?

   B: They take their break **at 3:30**.

4. *A:* _____ do they pay an hour?

   B: They pay **$12 an hour**.

5. *A:* _____ benefits do they offer?

   B: They offer **sick leave and vacation days**.

6. *A:* _____ does she get to school?

   B: She **drives her car**.

7. *A:* _____ do I apply?

   B: You **fill out an application online**.

8. *A:* _____ does he go home early?

   B: He goes home early **because he starts work early**.

4 **WHAT ABOUT YOU?** What job benefits are important to you? Circle 1 (*very important*), 2 (*important*), or 3 (*not important*).

1. Good salary	1	2	3	5. Vacation pay	1 2 3	
2. Overtime pay	1	2	3	6. Health insurance	1 2 3	
3. Safe working conditions	1	2	3	7. Sick leave benefits	1 2 3	
4. Nice employee lounge	1	2	3	8. Nice manager	1 2 3	

A good salary is very important to me.

TALK to a partner about your answers.

LESSON 5: Grammar Practice Plus

1 WRITE the words for job requirements under the pictures.

college degree	GED certificate	high school diploma
job training certificate	state license	union membership

GED certificate

_____

_____

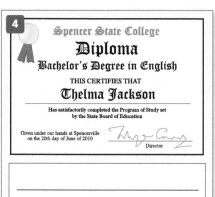

_____

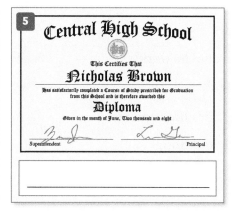

_____

_____

LISTEN and repeat. Are your answers correct?

TCD2, 11

2 WRITE. Complete the conversations. Use *do* or *does*.

1. *A:* How much education _____ *do* _____ I need for the manager position?

   B: You need a college degree.

2. *A:* _____ he need a high school diploma or GED certificate for this job?

   B: Yes, he _____ .

3. *A:* How _____ I apply?

   B: You fill out an application online.

4. *A:* When _____ Sally get her training certificate?

   B: After she finishes six months of training.

3 **WRITE** the words in the correct place in the chart.

repair computers	driver's license	two year's experience	assist doctors
health insurance	high school diploma	sick leave	computer skills
take care of children	overtime pay	college degree	supervise workers
vacation days	good salary	inspect luggage	help customers

Job Requirements	Job Responsibilities	Job Benefits
	repair computers	

4 **WHAT ABOUT YOU?** Think about the job you have or a job you want. Write your answers.

1. What job do you have or want? _____

2. What are the job responsibilities? _____

3. How much experience do you need? _____

4. What are the job requirements? _____

Math: Calculate Pay

Complete the form below.

1. Total regular pay: 40 x $11.00 = _____

2. Total overtime pay: 12 x $16.50 = _____

3. Total pay earned: _____
   (total regular pay + total overtime pay)

4. Total pay for week: _____
   (total pay earned – deductions)

MAIN STREET MANAGEMENT COMPANY
Employee Name: Bill Smith
Pay Period: February 1 through February 8

Hours	
Regular Hours	40 at $11.00 per hr
Overtime Hours	12 at $16.50 per hr
Pay	
Total regular pay	
Total overtime pay	
Total earned	
Deductions (taxes, health insurance)	– $127.60
Total Pay for Week	

LESSON 6: Apply Your Knowledge

1 **READ** the job ads. Write the abbreviations next to the words.

A

Wanted: Assistant Cook

F/T position in busy
restaurant; 1 yr exp;
Start immed; $12 hr; gd
ben w/ health ins.

Call 589-9844 to apply.

_____

B

Cashier

P/T nights and weekends;
need H.S. diploma; no exp req;
$8.50 hr; no ben.

Apply in person at Gas Mart
918 43rd St.

_____

C

Auto Salesperson

Ex sal w/ben; College degree
and 2 yrs exp req.

Apply online @
www.floridaauto.com

_____

benefits _____	good _____	insurance _____	with _____
excellent _____	high school _____	part-time _____	year _____
experience _____	hour _____	required _____	
full-time _____	immediately _____	salary _____	

2 **WRITE.** Answer the questions about the ads above. Write a question mark (?) for information *not* in the ads.

	A	B	C
1. What is the position advertised?	assistant cook		
2. Does the company offer benefits?	yes		
3. How much does the job pay?	$12 hr.		
4. Does the schedule include weekends?	?		
5. How much experience do you need?			
6. How do you apply?			

TCD2, 12

3 **LISTEN** to the phone conversation about each job ad. Take notes on the new information.

1. Ad **A**	Work schedule	includes weekends
2. Ad **B**	When does the job begin?	
3. Ad **C**	Work schedule	
	When does the job begin?	

4 **LISTEN** and read.

TCD2, 13
SCD, 24

A: Good morning. Big Steak Restaurant.

B: Good morning. My name is Susie Feng. I'm calling about the assistant manager position. I have a few questions.

A: Sure.

B: What are the job responsibilities?

A: The assistant manager trains the servers and plans the work schedule.

B: Do you offer benefits?

A: Yes, we offer sick leave, health insurance, and one week of vacation.

B: Okay. Thank you for the information.

TCD2, 14

LISTEN AGAIN and repeat. Then practice with a partner.

5 **PRACTICE THE CONVERSATION** with a partner. Use your own name.

1

assistant chef/make salads and assist the chef

2

chef/plan and cook dinners

3

kitchen manager/train workers and plan the work schedule for kitchen helpers

4

dining manager/ supervise servers and plan large parties

6 **TALK** with a partner. Call about the job opening. Then change roles and repeat.
Student A: Ask questions, listen to the answers, and take notes in the chart below. Write only the important words. **Student B:** Turn to page 198.

Job opening: Sales Manager at Spencer Auto Sales	
Job responsibilities	Train sales people, make work schedule
Experience	2 years
Salary	
Work schedule	
Benefits	
How/apply	

LESSON 7: Reading

1 THINK ABOUT IT. How do people apply for jobs in the United States? How do people apply for jobs in another country you know? Do they fill out an application? Do they talk to the business owner? Do they apply online?

Reading Tip

Scan (read quickly) when you are looking for specific information.

2 BEFORE YOU READ. Read the question. Scan the application. Check ☑ the answer.

What job does Teresa have now?

☐ childcare assistant ☐ teacher's assistant ☐ salesperson

3 READ the application. Find the words below and circle them.

signature work experience education

APPLICATION FOR EMPLOYMENT

PERSONAL INFORMATION

Name		
Gomez	Teresa	L
Last	First	Middle Initial

Address		City	State	Zip Code
5932 Landis Street		San Diego	CA	92105

Phone no. (619) 843-4893	Email address Tgomez61@mail.com

Are you 18 years or older? __X__ Yes _____ No	Social Security Number 123-45-6789

Sex _____ Male __X__ Female	Do you have a driver's license? _____ Yes __X__ No	If yes, what state?

EMPLOYMENT

Position desired Child Care Assistant	Check one: __X__ Full–time ____ Part–time	When can you work? __X__ Day ___ Night ___ Weekends

EDUCATION: Years of school 0 1 2 3 4 5 6 7 8 9 10 11 (12) 13 14 15

WORK EXPERIENCE (Write current or most recent experience first.)

From	To	Employer	Position
Jan 2005	present	Lincoln Elementary School, Chula Vista, California	Teacher's Assistant
Feb 1999	Mar 2003	Maria Bonita Clothing Shop, Mexico City, Mexico	Salesperson

Signature Teresa L. Gomez	Date: July 10

4 TALK. Read the questions. Share your answers with a partner.

1. What job does she want?

2. Does she have a driver's license?

3. Does she have experience?

4. Does she want a full-time job?

5. How many years of education does she have?

Writing

1 **WRITE.** Complete the application. Use your own information.

Writing Tip

1. Always use a pen for an application. Print carefully or complete on a computer.
2. Check all of your information very carefully.
3. Check for correct spelling and capital letters.

APPLICATION FOR EMPLOYMENT

PERSONAL INFORMATION

Name

Last	First	Middle Initial

Address	City	State	Zip Code

Phone no.	Email address

Are you 18 years or older? _____ Yes _____ No	Social Security Number

Sex _____ Male _____ Female	Do you have a driver's license? _____ Yes _____ No	If yes, what state?

EMPLOYMENT

Position desired	Check one: __ Full–time __ Part–time	When can you work? __ Day __ Night __ Weekends

EDUCATION: Years of school 0 1 2 3 4 5 6 7 8 9 10 11 12 13 14 15

WORK EXPERIENCE (Write current or most recent experience first.)

From	To	Employer	Position

Signature   Date:

_____

2 **EDIT.** Look at your job application above. Circle *yes* or *no*.

1. Is your writing neat?   yes   no

2. Did you check your spelling and capital letters?   yes   no

3. Did you fill in all the blanks?   yes   no

4. Did your write your current or very recent job first?   yes   no

5. Did you sign your name and write today's date?   yes   no

Career Connection

1 **READ AND LISTEN.** Then practice with a partner.

TCD2, 15

Hello, Marvin. What are you doing?

I'm taking a break. I'm thinking about the manager's job.

1

Did you fill out the application?

Not yet. I can do that really fast. I'll do it tomorrow.

2

Did you already write your resume? Did you prepare for the interview?

No, I don't need to prepare. What about you?

3

Yes, I wrote my resume and I prepared for the interview.

Not me. The manager, Lena, thinks I'm great, and I have more experience than you.

4

2 **WRITE.** What did Oscar do to apply for the manager position?

1. *fill out application* _____

2. _____

3. _____

3 **WHAT ABOUT YOU?** What things can you do to get a new job?

Check Your Progress!

Skill	Circle the correct words.	Is it correct?
A. Ask and answer simple present *yes/no* questions.	1. **Do**/**Does** Bob and Larry work the night shift? 2. Does he **need**/**needs** computer skills for his job? 3. Does the job require a state license? **No, he doesn't.**/**Yes, it does.** 4. Does he have a high school diploma? **Yes, he does.**/**Yes, he is.**	☐ ☐ ☐ ☐

| | Number Correct | 0 | 1 | 2 | 3 | 4 |

Skill	Circle the correct words.	Is it correct?
B. Ask and answer information questions.	5. **Who**/**What** benefits does the company offer? 6. **Where**/**What** do the employees take their breaks? 7. **When**/**What** does the job begin? On Monday. 8. **How much**/**How** do I apply? Fill out an application.	☐ ☐ ☐ ☐

| | Number Correct | 0 | 1 | 2 | 3 | 4 |

Skill	Circle the correct words.	Is it correct?
C. Talk about job positions and job responsibilities.	9. The **manager**/**cashier** supervises workers. 10. The flight attendants **inspect luggage**/**help passengers**. 11. The gardener **takes care of plants**/**takes care of passengers**. 12. The cashier **serves food**/**collects money**.	☐ ☐ ☐ ☐

| | Number Correct | 0 | 1 | 2 | 3 | 4 |

Skill	Circle the correct words.	Is it correct?
D. Discuss job benefits and requirements.	13. I stay home when I'm sick, but the company pays me. I have **vacation days**/**sick leave**. 14. When I go to the doctor, I don't pay. I have **health insurance**/**sick leave**. 15. The **employee lounge**/**union** is a place for employees to take their breaks. 16. The GED is the same as a **college degree**/**high school diploma**.	☐ ☐ ☐ ☐

| | Number Correct | 0 | 1 | 2 | 3 | 4 |

COUNT the number of correct answers above. Fill in the circles.

Chart Your Success

Skill	Needs Practice	Needs Practice	Okay	Very Good	Excellent!
A. Ask and answer simple present *yes/no* questions.	⓪	①	②	③	④
B. Ask and answer information questions.	⓪	①	②	③	④
C. Talk about job positions and job responsibilities.	⓪	①	②	③	④
D. Discuss job benefits and requirements.	⓪	①	②	③	④

LESSON 1: Grammar and Vocabulary

 1 **GRAMMAR PICTURE DICTIONARY.** Listen and repeat.

TCD2, 16
SCD, 25

1
I (broke) my arm.

2
I went to the **emergency room**.
I didn't wait long. I got a **cast**.

3
Yong Jin **cut** his finger. It hurt, but he didn't cry.

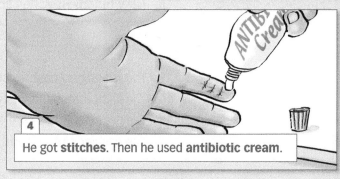

4
He got **stitches**. Then he used **antibiotic cream**.

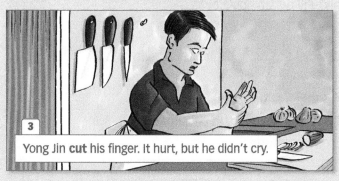

5
Luis **burned** his hand.

6
He applied **burn cream**. He didn't go to the emergency room.

7
Marie **sprained** her ankle. She put ice on it.

8
The doctor **examined** it and **wrapped** it in a **bandage**.

2 **NOTICE THE GRAMMAR.** Look at Activity 1. (Circle) the verbs. Underline *didn't*.

Simple Past Tense of Regular Verbs

We use the simple past tense to talk about actions completed in the past.

Affirmative		
Subject	Verb	
I You He She We You They	talked	to the doctor.

Negative			
Subject	*didn't*	Verb	
I You He She We You They	didn't	talk	to the nurse.

Spelling Rules

1. Add *-ed* or *-d* to most verbs. burn → burn**ed**, use → use**d**
2. If a verb ends in consonant + *y*, change the *y* to *i* and add *-ed*. stud**y** → stud**ied**
3. If a verb ends in vowel + *w*, *x*, or *y*, add *–ed*. sho**w** → show**ed**, fix → fix**ed**, sta**y** → stay**ed**
4. If a one-syllable verb ends in consonant + vowel + consonant, double the consonant and add *-ed*. s**top** → stop**ped**, sh**op** → shop**ped**

---

3 **WRITE** the past tense forms of the verbs.

1. walk _____ *walked* _____
2. try _____
3. play _____
4. fix _____
5. shop _____

6. call _____
7. start _____
8. wash _____
9. dance _____
10. mop _____

 **4** **WHAT ABOUT YOU?** Complete the sentences about you. Use the affirmative or negative past tense form of the verb in parentheses.

1. I _____ (play) a sport last weekend.
2. I _____ (shop) for food last week.
3. I _____ (talk) to my English teacher yesterday.
4. I _____ (walk) to English class last week.
5. I _____ (call) a doctor last week.

LESSON 2: Grammar Practice Plus

1 **LISTEN** and repeat.

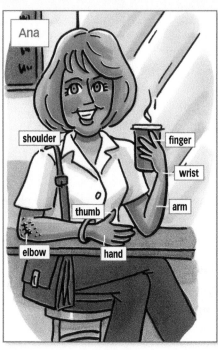

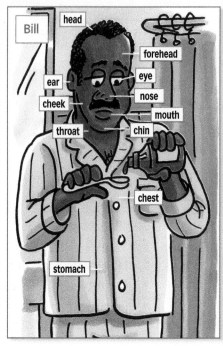

Irregular Verbs

Irregular verbs have special past tense forms. Do not add _-ed_ to irregular verbs in the past tense.

Present	Simple Past		Present	Simple Past		Present	Simple Past		Present	Simple Past
break	→ broke		fall	→ fell		go	→ went		make	→ made
catch	→ caught		feel	→ felt		have	→ had		put	→ put
cut	→ cut		get	→ got		hit	→ hit		see	→ saw
eat	→ ate		give	→ gave		hurt	→ hurt		take	→ took

*See page 208 for more irregular verbs.

2 **WRITE.** Complete the sentences about the people in Activity 1. Use body parts and the past tense forms of the verbs in parentheses.

1. Yesterday Ana _____*cut*_____ (cut) her _____*elbow*_____. She _____ (get) stitches. The doctor _____ (give) Ana a prescription for antibiotic cream.

2. Roberto _____ (fall) and _____ (hurt) his _____.

3. Otto _____ (have) a cold. He _____ (go) to the doctor. The doctor _____ (give) him a prescription for cough medicine.

3 **TALK** about the picture. What happened to the people?

4 **LISTEN** to the sentences. Circle *True* or *False*.

TCD2, 18

1. True   False   3. True   False   5. True   False

2. True   False   4. True   False   6. True   False

5 **TALK.** Look at the picture. The sentences below are not correct. Read the sentences.
Your partner corrects the sentences.

1. Martin sprained his ankle.   4. Minh hurt his knee.

2. Victor burned his finger.   5. Tom broke his arm.

3. Kim cut her arm.   6. Carrie hurt her head.

LESSON 3: Listening and Conversation

Pronunciation: Final sounds *t*, *d*, and *id*

A **READ** the examples.

Pronunciation Rules	Examples
1. For verbs ending in *b*, *l*, *n*, *v*, or a vowel sound, pronounce the *-d* like /d/.	called tried
2. For verbs ending in *ch*, *f*, *k*, *p*, *sh*, or *x*, pronounce the -ed like /t/.	talked stopped
3. For verbs ending in a *t* or *d* sound, pronounce the *-d* like /id/.	started needed

TCD2, 19
SCD, 26

B **LISTEN** and check ☑ the correct column. Then listen and repeat.

		t	d	id				t	d	id
1.	walked	☑	☐	☐		6.	washed	☐	☐	☐
2.	used	☐	☐	☐		7.	called	☐	☐	☐
3.	burned	☐	☐	☐		8.	waited	☐	☐	☐
4.	wanted	☐	☐	☐		9.	helped	☐	☐	☐
5.	wrapped	☐	☐	☐		10.	applied	☐	☐	☐

TCD2, 20
SCD, 27

C **LISTEN** and repeat.

1. I **call** the doctor.   I **called** the doctor.

2. I **use** burn cream.   I **used** burn cream.

3. I **wash** my hands.   I **washed** my hands.

4. I **wait** for the doctor.   I **waited** for the doctor.

TCD2, 21

1 **LISTEN** to the question. Then listen to the phone conversation. Fill in the correct answer.

1. Ⓐ Ⓑ Ⓒ

2. Ⓐ Ⓑ Ⓒ

3. Ⓐ Ⓑ Ⓒ

4. Ⓐ Ⓑ Ⓒ

TCD2, 22
SCD, 28

2 **LISTEN** and read.

A: City Medical Offices. How may I help you?

B: My name is Susan Chen. I'd like to make an appointment.

A: What's the problem?

B: I hurt my shoulder last week. The doctor wanted to check it again this week.

A: Okay. How about tomorrow, January 7, at 9:00 A.M.?

B: That's fine. Thank you.

A: See you then.

TCD2, 23

LISTEN AGAIN and repeat. Then practice with a partner.

3 **PRACTICE THE CONVERSATION** with a partner. Use your own name.

1

burned my arm/
December 20, 3:00 P.M.

2

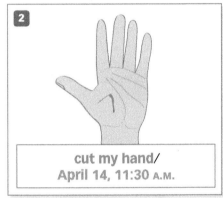

cut my hand/
April 14, 11:30 A.M.

3

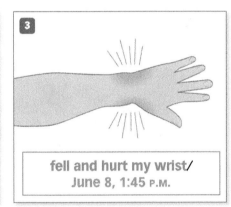

fell and hurt my wrist/
June 8, 1:45 P.M.

4

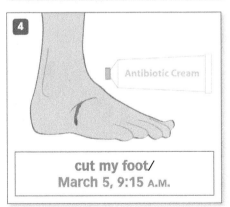

Antibiotic Cream

cut my foot/
March 5, 9:15 A.M.

5

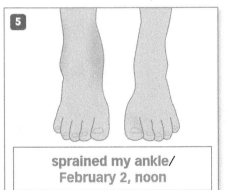

sprained my ankle/
February 2, noon

6

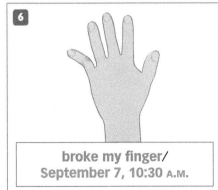

broke my finger/
September 7, 10:30 A.M.

4 **TALK** to a partner about injuries you had.

Last year I hurt my back.

Did you see a doctor?

LESSON 4: Grammar and Vocabulary

1 GRAMMAR PICTURE DICTIONARY. Listen and repeat.

TCD2, 24

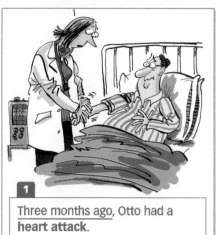

1 Three months ago, Otto had a **heart attack**.

2 Two months ago, Otto changed his **diet**. Now he eats healthy food.

3 Last month, Otto **lost five pounds**.

4 Last week, Otto went to the doctor for a **follow-up visit**.

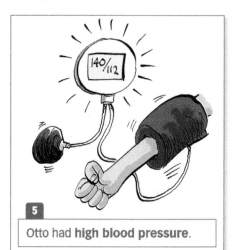

5 Otto had **high blood pressure**.

6 Otto got a **prescription**.

PRESCRIPTIONS

HIGH BLOOD PRESSURE MEDICATION

GYM

7 The day before yesterday, Otto **joined** a gym.

8 Last night he **exercised**.

9 This morning he woke up early. He felt **strong** and **energetic**!

2 NOTICE THE GRAMMAR. Look at Activity 1. Underline the past time words.

> Time expressions can come at the beginning or the end of a statement: **Last week** *I had an appointment.* **OR** *I had an appointment* **last week**.

Past Time Expressions

Time expressions tell when something happened.

	Past Time Expression
I had a doctor's appointment	on Tuesday. yesterday. three days ago.

Past Time Expressions		
this morning	at 8:00	last fall
yesterday	on Sunday	last winter
the day before yesterday	in June	last weekend
two days ago	in 2005	last month
three years ago	last summer	last year
		last night

3 **WRITE.** Complete the sentences with past time expressions.

1. Today is October 26th. _____*Yesterday*_____ was October 25th.

2. Today is Tuesday. _____ was Monday.

3. This year is 2010. _____ was 2009.

4. Today is Saturday. I had a doctor's appointment last Thursday. My appointment was

   _____ .

5. I came to this country in _____ . That was

   _____ .

6. It is 10:00 in the morning. I called my sister two hours ago. I called my sister

   _____ .

4 **WHAT ABOUT YOU?** Write sentences about you. Use past time expressions.

1. I came to this country _____ .

2. I started this class _____ .

3. I got up _____ .

4. I called someone in my family_____ .

TALK. Read your sentences with a partner.

LESSON 5: Grammar Practice Plus

1 **WRITE.** Complete the sentences. Use the words in the box.

allergies	asthma	cough
earache	headache	infection

Prescription Medications

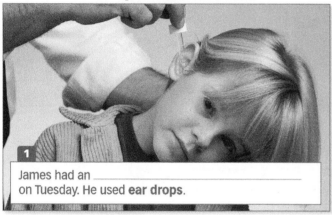

1
James had an _____ on Tuesday. He used **ear drops**.

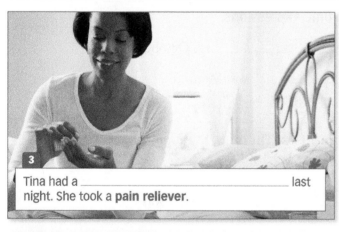

3
Tina had a _____ last night. She took a **pain reliever**.

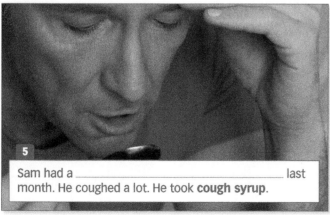

5
Sam had a _____ last month. He coughed a lot. He took **cough syrup**.

Over-the-Counter Medications
(medications you can buy without a prescription)

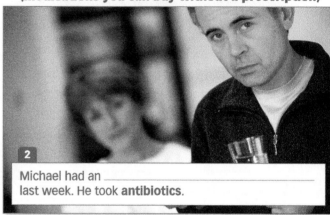

2
Michael had an _____ last week. He took **antibiotics**.

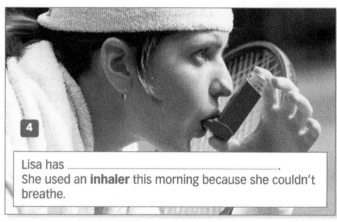

4
Lisa has _____.
She used an **inhaler** this morning because she couldn't breathe.

6
Ed has _____ in the spring and fall. He takes **antihistamines**.

2 **LISTEN** and repeat. Are your answers correct?

TCD2, 25

3 **LISTEN.** Lee is talking to the doctor about his family's medical history. Check ☑ the correct illnesses for each person.

Family Medical History				
	Lee's mother	When?	Lee's father	When?
1. Heart attack			✓	*last year*
2. High blood pressure				
3. Diabetes				
4. Asthma				

LISTEN AGAIN. In the chart, write when Lee's mother and father had the illnesses.

Math: Calculate Dosages

Read the medicine labels. Complete the sentences.

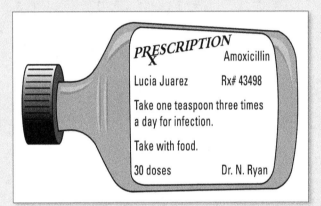

PRESCRIPTION Rx
Amoxicillin
Lucia Juarez   Rx# 43498
Take one teaspoon three times a day for infection.
Take with food.
30 doses   Dr. N. Ryan

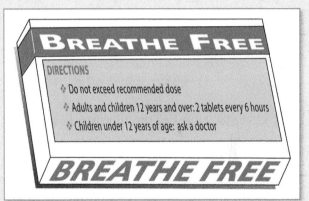

BREATHE FREE
DIRECTIONS
❖ Do not exceed recommended dose
❖ Adults and children 12 years and over: 2 tablets every 6 hours
❖ Children under 12 years of age: ask a doctor
BREATHE FREE

1. Lucia takes _____ teaspoons of amoxicillin three times a day.

2. She takes a total of _____ teaspoons of amoxicillin every day.

3. There are _____ doses of amoxicillin in the bottle. Lucia has medicine
   for _____ days.

4. Adults take _____ Breathe Free tablets every _____ hours.

5. Ed took a Breathe Free tablet at 1:00. He should take another tablet at _____ .

LESSON 6: Apply Your Knowledge

1 **READ.** Complete the sentences.

Scrub and Shine Bathroom Cleaner with Bleach

Warning: May cause skin irritation. Wear gloves when using.
Do not get in eyes. Do not drink.

FIRST-AID:

IF IN EYES: Wash eyes with warm water for 15 minutes.

IF SWALLOWED: Drink a large glass of water. Call 911 immediately.

1. Wear _____ when you use Scrub and Shine because it can cause _____ .

2. If Scrub and Shine gets in your eyes, wash your eyes with _____ for _____ .

3. If someone swallows Scrub and Shine, the person should _____ and call _____ .

2 **LISTEN.** Number the pictures in the correct order.

3 **WRITE.** Complete the sentences about the pictures above. Use the past tense forms of the verbs in the box.

1. A girl _____ kitchen cleanser.

2. Her mother _____ her milk to drink.

3. Her mother _____ 911.

call
give
swallow

4 **TALK** with a partner. Ask and answer the questions.

1. What did the mother do right?

2. What did the mother do wrong?

TCD2, 29
SCD, 29

5 **LISTEN** and read.

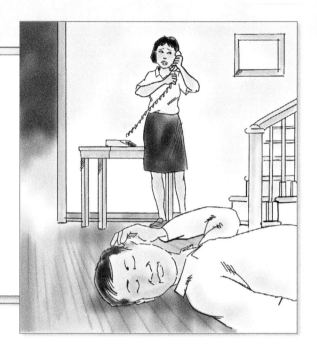

> A: 911. What's the address of the emergency?
>
> B: The address? 576 Grove Street.
>
> A: Okay. What's the problem?
>
> B: My husband fell and hit his head!
>
> A: Is he breathing?
>
> B: Yes, he's breathing, but he needs help.
>
> A: Okay. Don't hang up. An ambulance is coming.
>
> B: Thank you.

TCD2, 30

LISTEN AGAIN and repeat. Then practice with a partner.

6 **PRACTICE THE CONVERSATION** with a partner. Use your own name.

1

6589 Larkin Street/
My daughter fell and
hurt her head.

2

993 Park Street/
My husband is choking.

3

131 Macy Drive/My son
fell off of his skateboard.

7 **TALK.** Work with a partner. Fill in the blanks below. Then take turns being the doctor's receptionist or the 911 operator.

1. What is the emergency? _____

2. Should you call 911 or the doctor's office? _____

3. Have a conversation. Call 911 or the doctor's office and report a problem.

LESSON 7: Reading

1 **THINK ABOUT IT.** If you see someone choking, what should you do?

2 **BEFORE YOU READ.** Scan the story. Read the question. Circle the answer.

Where did the story happen?

A. in a school playground

B. at a home

C. in a classroom

> **Reading Tip**
>
> When you read a story, look for words that help you remember the **order of events**: *next, first, then, finally*.

3 **READ.** Circle these words: *first, then, next, finally*. Then choose the best title for the story.

A. Teenage Boy Saves Sister's Life

B. Young Boy Calls 911 to Save Sister's Life

C. Young Girl Saves Brother from Choking on a Toy

PORTLAND – Joey McCall, 15, saved his sister's life on Tuesday afternoon. Joey was at home alone with his three-year-old sister Marcy. At about 2:00, Joey was in the kitchen, and Marcy was in the living room. Marcy was very loud, but then she got very quiet. Joey ran into the living room to check on her. Her face was blue. She couldn't breathe. First, Joey looked in her mouth. He saw something green in the back of her throat. It was a small ball. Then, Joey put his arm across his sister's chest. Next he hit her on the back five times. Then the ball came out. Finally, Marcy coughed a little bit, but she was okay. Joey's mother said, "We are so thankful. Joey just learned about first aid and choking at school last week!"

4 **NUMBER** the events in the correct order.

_____ Marcy coughed a little.

_____ Joey hit Marcy on the back.

_____ Joey put his arm across Marcy's chest.

_____ The ball came out.

_1_ Joey looked into Marcy's mouth.

_____ Joey saw something in the back of Marcy's throat.

Writing

1 **NUMBER** the pictures in the correct order.

Last Monday, 5:30 P.M.

2 **WRITE.** You are the person in the pictures. Write sentences about
the accident.

1. What did you see?

   I saw a car accident.

2. What happened?

   _____

3. What did you do?

   _____

   _____

   _____

3 **WRITE** your sentences from Activity 2 in a paragraph. Indent the first line.

_____

_____

_____

_____

_____

Writing Tip

A paragraph is a group
of sentences about one
main idea. **Indent**, or
leave some space, at the
beginning of a paragraph.

1 READ AND LISTEN. Then practice with a partner.

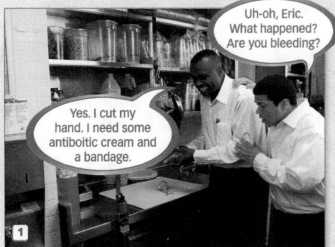

2 WRITE. Fill out Eric's accident report.

Employee's Name: _Eric Munson_ **Job:** _____

Where did the accident happen? _____ **When:** _Monday, 7:00 pm._

Describe the injury: _____

_____

Who saw the accident? _____

What first aid did you need? _____

 3 WHAT ABOUT YOU? Do you have a first-aid kit at home or at work? What's in the kit?

Check Your Progress!

Skill	Circle the correct words.	Is it correct?
A. Make statements in past tense.	1. I **break** / **broke** my arm yesterday. 2. He **went** / **wents** to the emergency room. 3. My daughter **cut** / **cuts** her finger last night. 4. She **didn't cried** / **didn't cry**.	☐ ☐ ☐ ☐
	Number Correct	0 1 2 3 4
B. Make statements with past time expressions.	5. I had a heart attack **two years ago** / **two ago years**. 6. Marvin had a bad cold **week last** / **last week**. 7. She had a doctor's appointment **on Tuesday** / **in Tuesday**. 8. Mary sprained her ankle **today morning** / **this morning**.	☐ ☐ ☐ ☐
	Number Correct	0 1 2 3 4
C. Read medicine labels.	9. The dosage is **for foot pain** / **two tablets every four hours**. 10. The **prescription number** / **phone number** is 79484. 11. The quantity is **ear drops** / **100 tablets**. 12. How many **prescriptions** / **doses** are in the bottle?	☐ ☐ ☐ ☐
	Number Correct	0 1 2 3 4
D. Report a medical emergency.	13. My husband **fell down** / **down fell** and hit his head. 14. Come quickly! The man is having a **heart attack** / **heart choke**! 15. The baby swallowed a toy. She's **falling** / **choking**. 16. My daughter cut her arm. It's **bleeding** / **breathing**.	☐ ☐ ☐ ☐
	Number Correct	0 1 2 3 4

COUNT the number of correct answers above. Fill in the circles.

Chart Your Success					
Skill	Needs Practice	Needs Practice	Okay	Very Good	Excellent!
A. Make statements in past tense.	⓪	①	②	③	④
B. Make statements with past time expressions.	⓪	①	②	③	④
C. Read medicine labels.	⓪	①	②	③	④
D. Report a medical emergency.	⓪	①	②	③	④

LESSON 1: Grammar and Vocabulary

1 **GRAMMAR PICTURE DICTIONARY** Listen and repeat.

TCD2, 32
SCD, 30

1
A: Did the **movers load** the truck?
B: Yes, they did.

2
A: Did the plumber **install** the sink?
B: Yes, she did.

3
A: Did the mechanics **repair** the car?
B: Yes, they did.

4
A: Did the **computer technician help** the customer?
B: Yes, she did.

5
A: Did the **delivery person deliver** the package?
B: Yes, he did.

6
A: Did the salesperson **sell** a shirt?
B: No, she didn't. She sold a jacket.

7
A: Did the **carpenter build** a table?
B: No, he didn't. He built a bookcase.

8
A: Did the **stockperson stock** the shelves?
B: Yes, she did.

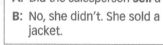

9
A: Did she pay the **repairperson**?
B: Yes, she did. She paid him $87.00.

2 **NOTICE THE GRAMMAR.** Look at Activity 1. <u>Underline</u> *did* and the base form of the verb.

Simple Past Tense: *Yes/No* Questions and Answers

We use simple past questions to ask about actions in the past.

Question					Affirmative					Negative			
Did	**Subject**	**Verb**				**Subject**	**did**				**Subject**	**did + not**	
	I					I					I		
	you					you					you		
	he					he					he		
Did	she	load	the boxes?		Yes,	she	did.			No,	she	didn't.	
	we					we					we		
	you					you					you		
	they					they					they		

---

3 **WRITE.** Complete the questions and answers. Use the verbs in the box.

1. *A:* Did the plumber _____*repair*_____ your leaky toilet?

   B: Yes, he _____ .

2. *A:* Did you _____ the shelves with cans of soup?

   B: No, I _____ .

3. *A:* Did the plumber _____ the new sink?

   B: Yes, she _____ .

4. *A:* Did the delivery person _____ the package this morning?

   B: No, he _____ .

5. *A:* Did the movers _____ the boxes onto the truck?

   B: Yes, they _____ .

~~repair~~
load
stock
install
help
deliver

4 **WHAT ABOUT YOU?** Talk to a partner. Ask what he or she did last night.

1. study

2. watch TV

3. read

4. cook dinner

5. talk on the phone

Did you study last night?

Yes, I did. I studied English.

LESSON 2: Grammar Practice Plus

1 **WRITE** questions and answers. Use the past tense.

repair – repaired	make – made	give – gave	bring – brought

1. (the office assistant / make copies)

A: _Did the office assistant make copies?_

B: Yes, he ____did____ . He ____made____ six copies.

2. (maintenance person / repair the window)

A: _____

B: No, he _____ . He _____ the door.

3. (the housekeeper / make the beds)

A: _____

B: Yes, she _____ . She _____ beds in 16 rooms.

4. (the cashier / give change)

A: _____

B: Yes, she _____ . She _____ the customer $1.67.

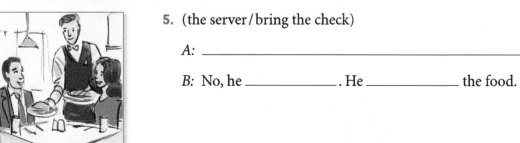

5. (the server / bring the check)

A: _____

B: No, he _____ . He _____ the food.

Answer *yes / no* questions. • Learn job titles.

2 **WRITE.** Look at the words in Activity 3. Then write the number next to the correct person in the art.

He's a stockperson.

3 **LISTEN.** Check your answers. Were you correct?

| 1. housekeeper | 2. painter | 3. salesclerk | 4. stockperson |
| 5. chef | 6. plumber | 7. delivery person | 8. carpenter |

4 **TALK.** Work with a partner. Ask and answer questions about what happened yesterday at the hotel.

1. the housekeeper / vacuum / the floor
2. the plumber / fix the sink
3. the stockperson / stock / the magazines
4. the salesclerk / sell / a book
5. the painter / paint / the wall
6. the carpenter / repair / the door

7. the chef / prepare / the dinner
8. the delivery person / deliver / the boxes

Did the housekeeper make the bed?

Yes, she did.

LESSON 3: Listening and Conversation

Pronunciation: Intonation of Yes/No Questions

 A **LISTEN** and repeat.

TCD2, 34
SCD, 31

A: Did you make the beds?

B: Yes, I did.

A: Did you vacuum the floors?

B: Yes, I did.

A: Did you clean all the rooms?

B: Yes, I did. I worked all day.

B **PRACTICE** the conversation with a partner.

---

 1 **LISTEN** to the question. Then listen to three possible answers to finish the conversation. Fill in the correct answer.

TCD2, 35

1. Ⓐ   Ⓑ   Ⓒ   3. Ⓐ   Ⓑ   Ⓒ

2. Ⓐ   Ⓑ   Ⓒ   4. Ⓐ   Ⓑ   Ⓒ

---

 2 **LISTEN.** Circle the correct answer.

TCD2, 36

Why is Mark calling Amina?

A. He wants to know what Amina did today.

B. He is sick. He can't come to work.

C. Mark wants to talk about Amina's schedule next week.

---

 3 **LISTEN AGAIN.** Check ☑ the things Amina did at work today.

TCD2, 37

To-Do List	Date: _____5/17_____
☐ Write pay checks	☐ Call Mr. Jones
☐ Make copies of pay checks	☐ Send package to Mrs. Green
☐ Check email	☐ Take letters to post office

4 **LISTEN** and read.

TCD2, 38
SCD, 32

A: What did you do today?

B: I installed a new engine in Mr. Tan's car.

A: Did you finish the repairs on Mrs. Johnson's car?

B: No, I didn't. I didn't have time.

A: That's okay. You can do that tomorrow.

TCD2, 39 **LISTEN AGAIN** and repeat. Then practice with a partner.

5 **PRACTICE THE CONVERSATION** with a partner.

1

paint the living room /
repair the walls

2

build a bookcase /
install the new door

3

pay the bills /
call customers about their orders

6 **WHAT ABOUT YOU?** Write questions about your partner's activities before class today. Then ask the questions.

A: Did you check email?

B: No, I didn't.

A: Did you call a friend?

B: Yes, I did.

1. Did you _____

2. Did you _____

3. Did you _____

4. Did you _____

LESSON 4: Grammar and Vocabulary

1 **GRAMMAR PICTURE DICTIONARY.** Listen and repeat.

1
A: (How) did you **find out** about this position?
B: I read about it online.

2
A: Where did you work before this job?
B: I worked at a **computer software** company.

3
A: What did you do at your last job?
B: I **designed** websites.

4
A: Who did you **report** to?
B: I reported to the manager.

5
A: Why did you **leave** your last job?
B: I left because I moved to a new town.

6
A: When did you get your **degree**?
B: I got my degree five years ago.

2 **NOTICE THE GRAMMAR.** Look at Activity 1. (Circle) the question words. Underline *did* and the base verb in each question.

Ask and answer simple past tense questions about work history.

Simple Past Tense: Information Questions

Use question words to ask for information about the past.

Questions

Question Word	did	Subject	Verb	
How	did	I	do?	
When	did	you	leave	your last job?
Where	did	he/she	learn	to drive?
What	did	we	forget	to do at work?
Who	did	you	ask	to the party?
Why	did	they	leave	their jobs?

Answers

Subject	Verb	
You	did	very well.
I	left	my last job in March.
He/She	learned	to drive in Mexico.
You	forgot	to repair the window.
We	asked	the manager.
They	left	because of the pay.

3 WRITE. Put the words in the correct order to make questions. Then write the answers.

1. when / you / start / this job / did

   A: _When did you start this job?_

   B: I _____started_____ this job last month.

2. they / how / do / did

   A: _____

   B: They _____ very well.

3. she / degree / her / where / get / did

   A: _____

   B: She _____ her degree at UCLA.

4 WHAT ABOUT YOU? Complete the questions. Use the verbs in parentheses.

1. What _____did_____ you _____do_____ (do) last Saturday?

2. Where _____ you _____ (go) last weekend?

3. When _____ you _____ (arrive) at school today?

4. How _____ you _____ (get) to school today?

5. What _____ you _____ (have) for breakfast today?

TALK. Ask and answer the questions with a partner.

go–went	do–did	get–got	have–had	arrive–arrived

LESSON 5: Grammar Practice Plus

1 READ the interview tips. Number the tips to show the correct order.

Interview Tips

- _____ When you meet the interviewer, **make eye contact**. Look at the interviewer's eyes. Don't look down.

- _____ During the interview, **ask questions** about the job and about the company.

- _____ **Dress neatly** for your interview. Wear clean, nice clothes.

- _____ After your interview, **send a thank-you note**. You can mail a card or send an email. This tells the interviewer you really want the job.

- _1_ First **prepare** before your interview. Learn about the company. Think of questions to ask. Think of answers to questions the interviewer will ask you.

- _____ **Arrive on time** or early for your interview. Don't be late.

Prepare before your interview.

Make eye contact.

2 TALK. Look at the pictures below. Ask and answer the questions with a partner.

1. What did Kate wear to her interview?

2. What time did Kate arrive? Did she arrive early or late?

3. How did she do in her interview?

4. What did she do right?

5. What did she do wrong?

3 LISTEN to the interview. Then read the sentences. Check ☑ *True* or *False*.

TCD2, 41

	True	False
1. Jack delivered refrigerators and ovens at his last job.	☐	☐
2. Jack repaired refrigerators and ovens at his last job.	☐	☐
3. Jack reported to the assistant manager.	☐	☐
4. Jack left his last job because he graduated.	☐	☐
5. Jack graduated four months ago.	☐	☐

4 TALK with a partner. Ask and answer questions about Jack and his interview. Use question words: *What, Where, When, Who, Why,* and *How.*

How did Jack do in his interview?

He did very well.

5 WHAT ABOUT YOU? Answer the questions. Then ask a partner the questions. Write your partner's answers.

1. Where was your last job? _____

   You: _____

   Partner: _____

2. Do you have a driver's license? _____

   You: _____

   Partner: _____

3. When did you learn to drive? _____

   You: _____

   Partner: _____

4. What time did you arrive at class? _____

   You: _____

   Partner: _____

5. Why did you leave your last job? _____

   You: _____

   Partner: _____

LESSON 6: Apply Your Knowledge

1 **READ** the paragraph and the schedule. Circle the days when Otto's "scheduled" hours don't match his "worked" hours.

> Otto works part-time at Good Food Supermarket. He is an assistant manager. Last week, a co-worker was sick and Otto's boss asked him to work extra hours. The schedules show Otto's usual hours and the extra hours he worked last week.

Otto's Usual Work Schedule

Monday	Tuesday	Wednesday	Thursday	Friday
9:00–4:00 (Lunch 12:00–1:00)	8:30–5:30 (Lunch 12:30–1:30)	12:00–3:00	DAY OFF	12:00–4:00

Actual hours Otto worked last week

9:00–3:00 (Lunch 12:00–1:00)	8:30–4:30 (Lunch 12:00–1:00)	8:00–3:00 (Lunch 12:00–1:00)	9:00–7:00 (Lunch 12:00–1:00)	10:00–7:00 (Lunch 12:00–1:00)

2 **LISTEN** to the questions. Circle the correct answers.

TCD2, 42

1. **A.** Yes, he did.   **B.** No, he didn't.   4. **A.** At 4:00.   **B.** At 7:00.

2. **A.** Yes, he did.   **B.** No, he didn't.   5. **A.** 8 hours.   **B.** 9 hours.

3. **A.** At 9:00.   **B.** At 3:00.   6. **A.** Yes, he did.   **B.** No. he didn't.

Math: Calculate hours on a work schedule

Look at Otto's usual work schedule and the actual hours Otto worked last week. Answer the questions.

1. How many hours does Otto usually work each week? _____

2. How many hours did Otto work last week? _____

3. How many extra hours did Otto work because his co-worker was sick? _____

3 **LISTEN** and read.

TCD2, 43
SCD, 33

A: How many hours did you work last week?

B: I worked 25 hours last week.

A: What days did you work?

B: I worked Monday through Friday.

A: Did you work nights?

B: Yes, I worked two nights.

TCD2, 44

LISTEN AGAIN and repeat. Then practice with a partner.

4 **PRACTICE THE CONVERSATION** from Activity 3 with a partner.

1	2	3
30 hours/ Monday through Friday/ three nights	18 hours/ Tuesday, Thursday, Friday, and Saturday/ one night	40 hours/ Tuesday through Saturday/ no nights

4	5	6
24 hours/ Monday, Wednesday, and Friday/ two nights	30 hours/ Thursday through Sunday/ no nights	12 hours/ Friday and Saturday/ two nights

5 **PUT IT TOGETHER.** Talk with a partner. **Student A:** ask your partner questions about Martin's schedule. Fill in the missing information. **Student B:** look at page 198. Answer your partner's questions about Martin's work schedule.

Employee: *Martin Salcedo*				Date:
Monday	**Tuesday**	**Wednesday**	**Thursday**	**Friday**
9:00–4:00 *(Lunch 12:00–1:00)*		*10:00–5:00* *(Lunch 1:00–2:00)*	*Day Off*	

Total hours: _____

LESSON 7: Reading

1 THINK ABOUT IT. What makes you happy? Are you happy at work? What kind of job can make you happy?

2 BEFORE YOU READ. Look at the title. What do you think this article is about?

A. How to earn a lot of money.

B. How to find a good husband or wife.

C. How to find a good job for you.

> **Reading Tip**
>
> **Take notes** when you read. You can note what the main idea of each paragraph is. This will help you remember information.

3 READ. <u>Underline</u> the questions about you and jobs in the article. Take notes on the main idea of each paragraph.

Find the *Job You LOVE*

Finding a job is hard work. It's even harder to find a job you love. Here are some tips to help you find a job you can love for a long time.

1. *Ask yourself important questions.* What makes you happy? Do you like to work alone or with people? Do you like to work inside or outside? Make a list of questions and write answers to the questions.

2. *Make a list of your skills and experience.* What do you do well? Ask family and friends to help you make a list of things you do well. What experience do you have? If you did not work before, what did you do at home or in the community? Did you take care of children? Maybe you can work in a child care center. Did you help your father on the farm? Maybe you can work as a gardener. Did you cook dinner for your family? Maybe you can work in a restaurant.

3. *Get information about jobs.* Read newspaper ads, use the Internet, talk to friends who have jobs. Learn all you can about a lot of different jobs. Write the information. Think about the job responsibilities. Are the job responsibilities things you like to do? How much does the job pay? Can you pay your bills and have a little extra money to save or have fun? That's the job you can love for a long time.

4. *Get experience.* Volunteer in your child's class, at your own school, at the hospital or other place in the community. It's very helpful to have experience. If you don't have job experience, volunteer experience can help you get a job.

5. *Think happy thoughts.* When you THINK you can do something, you CAN.

---

4 READ AGAIN. What is the main idea of the article?

A. You can find a job you love.

B. You need to get information about jobs.

C. Jobs are always fun.

Writing

1 **THINK ABOUT IT.** What job is interesting for you? What questions do you have about the job?

2 **BEFORE YOU WRITE.** Answer the questions. If you didn't have a job before, write about work you did in your home, at school, or in the community.

1. When are you happy? I am happy when I _____
_____

2. Do you like to work alone or with people? I like to work _____

3. What do you do well? I _____ very well.

4. What work did you do in your country for your job or for your family? _____
_____

5. What do you do now? _____

6. What job do you think you can love? I think I can love a job as a _____
_____

3 **WRITE** a paragraph. Copy your sentences from Activity 2. Use the sample paragraph below as a model.

> I am looking for a job I can love. I am happy when I work outside. I like to work alone. I take care of plants very well. In my country I worked on my father's farm. Now I go to school and I work in my garden. I plant vegetables and flowers. I think I can love a job as a gardener.

_____

_____

_____

_____

_____

_____

Writing Tip

Every sentence in your paragraph should begin with a capital letter and have a punctuation mark at the end. Check each for sentence **capitalization** and **punctuation**.

Career Connection

1 READ AND LISTEN. Then practice with a partner.

1. **Lena:** Oscar, sorry you had to wait. Marvin was late for his interview and now I'm late for all my interviews.

   Oscar: No problem, Lena. Thank you for meeting with me.

2. **Lena:** You worked as an assistant stock manager in a store. What did you do in that position?

   Oscar: I took care of and scheduled deliveries. I also supervised two stock clerks.

3. **Lena:** Great! Tell me about yourself. Why do you want to be manager of this restaurant?

   Oscar: Well, I really enjoy working with people. I'm a hard worker. I want to make the restaurant very successful!

4. **Oscar:** Thank you for this interview, Lena.

   Lena: You have excellent qualifications, Oscar. Thanks for your time. I'll make my decision soon.

2 TALK AND WRITE.

1. Oscar had to wait for his interview. Why?

2. Do you think Oscar could be a good restaurant manager? Why or why not?

3. Write two qualifications Oscar has for the manager position.

   _____

   _____

3 WHAT ABOUT YOU? What job do you want? What qualifications do you have for that job?

Discuss employment qualifications.

Check Your Progress!

Skill	Circle the correct words.	Is it correct?				
A. Ask and answer questions in past tense.	1. Did the plumber **installs**/**install** the sink? 2. Did the mechanics **repaired**/**repair** the car? 3. Did the carpenter build the table? **Yes, he does.**/**Yes, he did.** 4. Did we pay the repairperson? **Yes, we did.**/**No, we did.**	☐ ☐ ☐ ☐				
	Number Correct	0	1	2	3	4
B. Ask and answer information questions in past tense.	5. **How many**/**When** hours did you work this week? I worked 22 hours. 6. **Where**/**Why** did you work before this job? I worked at ABC Software. 7. When did you arrive in this country? **San Francisco.**/**In July, 2006.** 8. What did you have for breakfast today? **I eat coffee and toast.**/**I ate juice and eggs.**	☐ ☐ ☐ ☐				
	Number Correct	0	1	2	3	4
C. Answer job interview questions.	9. Why did you leave your last job? **I painted cabinets.**/**I moved.** 10. What did you do at your last job? **I read about it online.**/**I designed websites**. 11. Who did you report to at your last job? **The manager.**/**I was a carpenter.** 12. When did you graduate from school? **I studied computer repair.**/**Five months ago.**	☐ ☐ ☐ ☐				
	Number Correct	0	1	2	3	4
D. Report completed work on the job.	13. Did you make the beds? **Yes, I do.**/**Yes, I did.** 14. Did you vacuum the floors? **No, I did.**/**No, I didn't.** 15. Did you make the copies? **Yes, I made 40 copies.**/**Yes, I make 40 copies.** 16. Did you finish the car repairs? **Yes, I didn't have time.**/**No, I didn't have time.**	☐ ☐ ☐ ☐				
	Number Correct	0	1	2	3	4

COUNT the number of correct answers above. Fill in the bubbles.

Chart Your Success					
Skill	Needs Practice	Needs Work	Okay	Very Good	Excellent!
A. Ask and answer questions in past tense.	⓪	①	②	③	④
B. Ask and answer information questions in past tense.	⓪	①	②	③	④
C. Answer job interview questions.	⓪	①	②	③	④
D. Report completed work on the job.	⓪	①	②	③	④

LESSON 1: Grammar and Vocabulary

1 **GRAMMAR PICTURE DICTIONARY.** Listen and repeat.

TCD3, 2
SCD, 34

1
A: How <u>was</u> your vacation?
B: It was **great**!

2
A: How was the weather?
B: It was **beautiful**.

3
A: How was your hotel?
B: It was very **comfortable**.

4
A: How was your **flight**?
B: It was **awful**.

5
A: Why was it awful?
B: There was a bad storm.
   I was **nervous**.

6
A: Was your wife nervous, too?
B: No, she wasn't. She was **calm**.

7
A: How was your train trip?
B: It was **pretty good**.

8
A: How were your kids?
B: They were **excited**. It was
   their first trip.

9
A: Were the seats comfortable?
B: No, they weren't. They were
   uncomfortable.

2 **NOTICE THE GRAMMAR.** Look at Activity 1. Underline *was* and circle *were*.

Simple Past of *Be*: Statements and Questions

Use the simple past tense of *be* to talk about things that started and ended in the past.

Affirmative Statements

Subject	*was/were*	
I	was	uncomfortable. excited. calm. nervous.
You	were	
She	was	
We	were	

Negative Statements

Subject	*was/were not*	
I	wasn't	uncomfortable. excited. calm. nervous.
You	weren't	
She	wasn't	
We	weren't	

Yes/No Questions

Was/Were	Subject	
Was	I	late? angry? in L.A. last month?
Was	he	
Were	you	

Information Questions

Question Word	*was/were*	Subject	
What	was	his	job?
Why	were	you	late?
When	were	you	in Spain?
Where	was	he	today?
Who	was	she	with?
How	was	your	trip?

3 **CIRCLE** the correct form of the verb.

1. Anna and Sofia **was /** (**were**) excited to come to the United States.

2. **Was / Were** your sisters in the United States last year?

3. Where **was / were** your hotel?

4. How **was / were** your parents?

5. When **was / were** your brother in Mexico?

6. I **wasn't / weren't** nervous.

4 **WHAT ABOUT YOU?** Write answers.

1. When was your last trip? _____

2. Where did you go? _____

3. Who was with you on your trip? _____

4. Was the trip good? _____

TALK. Ask and answer the questions with a partner.

LESSON 2: Grammar Practice Plus

1 **WRITE.** Look at the pictures. Put the words in order to make questions. Then write the answers.

Miami

Chicago

San Francisco

San Diego

1. *Q:* it / in Miami / sunny / Was _Was it sunny in Miami?_____

   A: _____

2. *Q:* foggy / was / it / Where _____

   A: _____

3. *Q:* the weather / How / in Chicago / was _____

   A: _____

4. *Q:* it / Was / in San Diego / freezing _____

   A: _____

LISTEN and repeat. Are your answers correct?

TCD3, 3

2 **WRITE.** Complete the sentences with *was, were, wasn't,* or *weren't.*

   A: Hi! Welcome back! Did you have a good flight?

   B: Yes, I did. It _____ great!

   A: _____ the food good?

   B: Yes, it _____, and the flight attendants _____ very

   friendly. But the seats _____ comfortable.

3 **LISTEN** and write the names in the picture.

Terry	Pat	Logan	Jamie

4 **WRITE.** Complete the questions. Use *was* or *were*. Then answer the questions.

1. _____Was_____ Logan comfortable? _____No, she wasn't._____

2. _____ Logan and Pat uncomfortable? _____

3. _____ Terry nervous? _____

4. _____ the weather windy outside? _____

5. _____ the dog calm? _____

6. _____ Jamie happy? _____

5 **WRITE** questions about the picture. Use the past tense of *be*.

1. Why _____was Pat nervous_____?   4. How _____?

2. Why _____?   5. How _____?

3. Was Logan _____?   6. _____ the dog _____?

TALK. Work with a partner. Ask and answer the questions.

LESSON 3: Listening and Conversation

Pronunciation: *Was he/she/it*

A **LISTEN** and repeat the questions.

TCD3, 5
SCD, 35

Was he /wuz ze/	Was she /wuz she/	Was it /wuz it/
Was he there?	Was she there?	Was it there?
Was he late?	Was she late?	Was it late?

B **LISTEN** and circle the word you hear: *he, she,* or *it*.

TCD3, 6
SCD, 36

1. Was **he** / **she** / **it** in class?
2. Was **he** / **she** / **it** early?
3. Was **he** / **she** / **it** worried?
4. Was **he** / **she** / **it** excited?
5. Was **he** / **she** / **it** in Dallas?
6. Who was **he** / **she** / **it** with?
7. Where was **he** / **she** / **it**?
8. Why was **he** / **she** / **it** nervous?

1 **LISTEN.** Circle the correct answer. Which picture shows the man you hear?

TCD3, 7

A

B

C

2 **LISTEN** to the question. Then listen to the conversation. Fill in the correct answer.

TCD3, 8

1. Ⓐ Ⓑ Ⓒ   4. Ⓐ Ⓑ Ⓒ
2. Ⓐ Ⓑ Ⓒ   5. Ⓐ Ⓑ Ⓒ
3. Ⓐ Ⓑ Ⓒ   6. Ⓐ Ⓑ Ⓒ

3 **LISTEN** and read.

A: How old were you when you came to this city?

B: I was 14 years old.

A: How did you feel?

B: I was nervous.

A: How did you get here?

B: I came by bus.

A: How was your trip?

B: It was exciting.

LISTEN AGAIN and repeat. Then practice with a partner.

4 **PRACTICE THE CONVERSATION** with a partner.

1 22 / afraid / train / awful

2 17 / happy / plane / short

3 39 / calm / car / long

4 50 / nervous / plane / okay

5 5 / excited / car / great

6 24 / worried / bus / very slow

5 **WHAT ABOUT YOU?** Ask a partner the questions. Take notes.

Questions	Notes
1. How old were you when you came to this country?	
2. How did you feel?	
3. How did you get here?	
4. How was your trip?	

LESSON 4: Grammar and Vocabulary

TCD3, 11
SCD, 38

1 **LISTEN** and repeat.

1 My new job is **more stressful** than my old job.

2 My old job was **more relaxed**.

3 My new salary is **higher**.

4 My old salary was **lower**.

5 The streets in this town are **quieter** than the streets in my hometown.

6 The streets in my **hometown** were **noisier** than the streets in my new town.

7 The buildings in my new town are **older** than the buildings in my hometown.

8 The buildings in my hometown were **newer** and **more modern**.

2 **NOTICE THE GRAMMAR.** Look at Activity 1. Underline the adjectives that end in -er. Circle the word *more* and the adjectives that come after *more*.

Comparative Adjectives

We use comparative adjectives to compare two nouns.

Adjective	Comparative Adjective
My old neighborhood was **noisy**.	My new neighborhood is **noisier**.

Using *than*

Subject + Verb	Comparative Adjective	*than*	Noun
My hometown was Houses in my new town are	bigger more expensive	than	my new town. houses in my hometown.

Rules	Examples
1. Add *-er* or *-r* to most **one-syllable adjectives.**	old**er** larg**er**
2. For most **one-syllable adjectives ending in consonant + vowel + consonant**, double the consonant and add *-er*. Do not double *w*.	big**ger** new**er**
3. For **two-syllable adjectives ending in *y***, change the *y* to *i* and add *-er*.	sunny ⟶ sunn**ier** noisy ⟶ nois**ier**
4. For **adjectives with two or more syllables that do *not* end in *y***, use the word *more*.	**more** relaxed **more** stressful
5. The adjectives *good* and *bad* are irregular.	good ⟶ **better** bad ⟶ **worse**

3 **WRITE.** Change each adjective to a comparative adjective.

1. slow _____ *slower* _____
2. hot _____
3. easy _____
4. smart _____
5. tall _____
6. good _____

7. foggy _____
8. excited _____
9. noisy _____
10. high _____
11. modern _____
12. sunny _____

4 **WHAT ABOUT YOU?** Talk with a partner. Compare two cities you know. Use *than*.

Dallas is bigger than Austin.

LESSON 5: Grammar Practice Plus

TCD3, 12

1 **LISTEN** and complete the chart below.

	100 Years Ago in New York City	Today in New York City
Average salary for workers	$_____ per year	$49,000 per year
Price of beef	10¢ a pound	$4.49 a pound
Population	_____ million	8.2 million

population: the number of people living in a place

Workers in New York City in 1907.

2 **WRITE.** Use the information in the chart in Activity 1 to complete the sentences. Use the comparative forms of the adjectives below.

large	high	~~low~~	small

1. The price of beef was _____lower_____ 100 years ago than it is today.

2. The average salary for workers is _____ now than it was 100 years ago.

3. The population of New York is _____ today than it was 100 years ago.

4. The population in New York was _____ 100 years ago than it is today.

> Remember to add a period (.) at the end of every statement and a question mark (?) after every question.

3 **WRITE** statements or questions about the information in Activity 1.

1. the population / higher / now / is

   The population is higher now. _____

2. New York City / more populated / today / 100 years ago / has / is / than it was

   _____

3. of beef / higher / the price / now / is

   _____

4. 100 years ago / smaller / was / the population / of New York

   _____

5. were / average salaries / for workers / lower / 100 years ago

   _____

4 **WRITE.** Put each adjective in the correct column. You can put some words in more than one column.

busy	expensive	noisy	large	calm	happy	old	tall
freezing	lazy	rainy	friendly	quiet	nervous	relaxed	windy

People	Cities	Weather
busy		

 5 **WHAT ABOUT YOU?** Write five sentences about you. Use comparative adjectives.

Examples: I'm <u>more handsome</u> than I was 10 years ago.

1. I'm _____ than I was ten years ago.

2. I'm _____ than I was ten years ago.

3. I'm _____ than I was ten years ago.

4. I'm _____ than I was ten years ago.

5. I'm _____ than I was ten years ago.

 6 **WHAT ABOUT YOU?** Write the comparative form of each adjective. Then ask the questions to a partner. Write *yes* or *no*.

Are you thinner than you were 10 years ago?

	Comparative	Are you . . .	Partner's answers
tall	*taller*	*Are you taller than you were 10 years ago?*	
happy			
busy			
nervous			
relaxed			

LESSON 6: Apply Your Knowledge

1 **READ.** Circle the comparative adjectives.

My name is Minh. I moved here two months ago. Before I moved, I looked at two different towns, Mitchell and Reston. Reston is a very small town. It is also very old. Mitchell is newer and the buildings are more modern. It's also larger and noisier than Reston. Reston is quieter than Mitchell, and I like quiet places. The rent for an apartment in Mitchell is more expensive than the rent in Reston. The rent for a two-bedroom apartment in Mitchell is $1,200 a month. A two-bedroom apartment in Reston is $800 a month. My family likes Reston. We think Reston is prettier than Mitchell. We think the schools in Reston are better, too. That's why we live in Reston.

TCD3, 13

2 **LISTEN** to the sentences. Circle *True* or *False* for each sentence.

1. True   False   3. True   False   5. True   False

2. True   False   4. True   False   6. True   False

Math: Say Large Numbers

When you say large numbers in English, say each group of numbers before or after a comma separately. The order of each group of numbers is million, thousand, hundred.

A **TALK.** Read the numbers to a partner.

3,152   three thousand, one hundred fifty-two

73,152   seventy-three thousand, one hundred fifty-two

8,473,152   eight million, four hundred seventy-three thousand, one hundred fifty-two

4,893   87,550   12,980,322

B **TALK.** Work with a partner. Student A, look at page 198. Read the sentences about Mitchell. Student B, write the numbers in the chart. Then, Student B, look at page 198. Read the sentences about Reston. Student A, write the numbers in the chart.

	Student A: Reston	Student B: Mitchell
Population		
Average salary		
Price of a 3-bedroom house		

3 **LISTEN** and read.

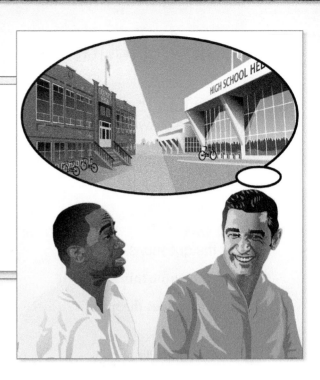

A: How do you like living in Baytown?

B: I like Baytown a lot. I lived in Midtown before. Baytown is nicer than Midtown.

A: How are the schools? Are they good?

B: The schools in Baytown are MUCH better than the schools in Midtown.

A: I am happy to hear that.

LISTEN AGAIN and repeat. Then practice with a partner.

TCD3, 15

4 **PRACTICE THE CONVERSATION** with a partner.

1 people/friendly

2 buildings/modern

3 food prices/cheap

4 neighborhood/quiet

5 rents/low

6 streets/clean

5 **WRITE** sentences. Compare Baytown and Midtown.

The schools are better in Baytown than they are in Midtown.

_____

_____

_____

LESSON 7: Reading

1 **THINK ABOUT IT.** Are your hometown and your new town similar or different? Write one or two words about how they are similar and how they are different.

similar: _____

different: _____

2 **BEFORE YOU READ.** Scan the article. Circle the correct answers for the questions.

a. Who wrote this article?   Boris Stevens   Steven Berkley

b. Where does the man live now?   His hometown   Riverton

3 **READ.** Underline the words and phrases that describe the two towns.

Riverton Adult Center News

Two Great Cities
By Steven Berkley

I like my new city, Riverton. It is very different from my hometown. My new city is larger and noisier than my hometown. It's also colder here. The supermarkets in Riverton are bigger, and the price of food is higher, but I think the food in my hometown was better. I miss the fresh vegetables I bought in open markets in my hometown! The air was cleaner in my hometown, too. But some things in my new city are similar to my hometown. Both cities are beautiful. Also, the people in both cities are very friendly. My hometown and my new city are both great cities!

---

4 **CHECK** ☑ the main idea of the article.

☐ **A.** Steven doesn't like his new city.

☐ **B.** Steven's new town is similar and different from his hometown.

☐ **C.** Steven's hometown was better than his new town.

5 **ORGANIZE** the information. Write the words you underlined in the article in the correct columns.

Steven's hometown	Both cities	Riverton
		larger

Writing

1 PLAN AHEAD. Answer the questions.

1. What is the name of your hometown? _____

2. What is the name of your city now? _____

2 BEFORE YOU WRITE. Think about the information you want to write. Write words, phrases, or sentences about your hometown and your city now in the columns below.

Writing Tip

Check your **spelling** carefully. Names of cities, countries, and people are very important. Make sure you spell these words correctly.

My hometown	Both cities	My new city

3 WRITE words and a sentence. Complete the paragraph. Write about your town now and your hometown.

My new town is different from my hometown. It is _____ than my hometown. It is also _____. My hometown is _____ than my new town. It is also _____. In some ways, my new town is similar to my hometown. Both cities are _____. _____

_____

4 WRITE. Copy the sentences from Activity 3 or make a new paragraph about your hometown and your new city.

_____

_____

_____

_____

_____

Career Connection

1 **READ AND LISTEN.** Then practice with a partner.

Eric, this is Sofia. She's our new server.

Nice to meet you, Sofia!

This is the kitchen. Watch out. When the chef gets upset, sometimes he throws tomatoes!

This kitchen is very clean. This is a really nice restaurant.

Sofia and I worked together in Florida! She just moved here a few weeks ago.

Wow, it's a small world! It's great to have a friend like Oscar here.

How do you like your new apartment and job?

I have a nicer apartment, a better schedule, and a higher salary. Life is great!

2 **CHECK** ✓ *yes* or *no*.

1. Sofia and Oscar worked together in Florida. ☐ yes ☐ no
2. Sofia is the new manager. ☐ yes ☐ no
3. Sofia has a better salary at her new job. ☐ yes ☐ no
4. The chef sometimes throws tomatoes. ☐ yes ☐ no

3 **WHAT ABOUT YOU?** Think about your life before and your life now. What is better about your life now? What is not better?

Check Your Progress!

Skill	Circle the correct words.	Is it correct?				
A. Make past tense statements with _be_.	1. He **was** / **is** tired last night. 2. Bob and Ana **was** / **were** excited about the trip. 3. I **was** / **were** nervous during the flight. 4. The weather **wasn't** / **weren't** good.	○ ○ ○ ○				
	Number Correct	0	1	2	3	4

Skill		Is it correct?				
B. Ask and answer past tense questions with _be_.	5. How **was** / **were** your flight? 6. **Were** / **Was** you excited? 7. Yes, I **were** / **was**. 8. No, she **weren't** / **wasn't**.	○ ○ ○ ○				
	Number Correct	0	1	2	3	4

Skill		Is it correct?				
C. Compare two cities.	9. Baytown is **large** / **larger** than Midtown. 10. Midtown is **more older than** / **older than** Baytown. 11. The schools in Midtown are **gooder** / **better** than the schools in Baytown. 12. The buildings in Baytown are **more modern** / **moderner** than the buildings in Midtown.	○ ○ ○ ○				
	Number Correct	0	1	2	3	4

Skill		Is it correct?				
D. Talk about your trip to the United States.	13. How old were you when you came to the U.S.? **I was 37.** / **I was tired.** 14. How did you feel? **I was tired.** / **He was excited.** 15. How did you get here? **I was nervous.** / **I came by car.** 16. How was the trip? **It weren't good.** / **It was good.**	○ ○ ○ ○				
	Number Correct	0	1	2	3	4

COUNT the number of correct answers above. Fill in the bubbles.

Chart Your Success					
Skill	Needs Practice	Needs Practice	Okay	Very Good	Excellent!
A. Make past tense statements with _be_.	⓪	①	②	③	④
B. Ask and answer past tense questions with _be_.	⓪	①	②	③	④
C. Compare two cities.	⓪	①	②	③	④
D. Talk about your trip to the United States.	⓪	①	②	③	④

LESSON 1: Grammar and Vocabulary

1 **GRAMMAR PICTURE DICTIONARY.** Listen and repeat.

TCD3, 17
SCD, 40

Count Nouns

1
a carrot

2
an egg

3
a few **bananas**
some bananas

4
several **lemons**

5
a lot of **blueberries**

6
two **steaks**
a couple of steaks

7
a couple of **onions**

8
some **peppers**

Non-Count Nouns

9
some **yogurt**

10
a lot of **garlic**

11
some **broccoli**

12
some **tuna**

13
a lot of **chicken**

14
a lot of **salt and pepper**

15
some **spinach**

16
some **coffee**

2 **NOTICE THE GRAMMAR.** Look at Activity 1. Circle the singular nouns. Underline the plural nouns.

Things we can count are called *count nouns*. Count nouns can be singular or plural: one egg, two eggs. *Non-count nouns* are always singular: coffee, salt.

Quantifiers

We use quantifiers to talk about the number or amount of something.

Quantifier	Count Noun
a	carrot
an	apple
two	oranges
a couple of	lemons
a few	peppers
some	eggs
several	onions
a lot of	bananas

Quantifier	Non-Count Noun
	protein
	spinach
	salt
a little bit of	coffee
some	tuna
a lot of	chicken
	cereal
	milk

3 **WRITE** a food item from Activity 1 in each box below. Add one more food item to each box. Then circle the non-count nouns and underline the count nouns.

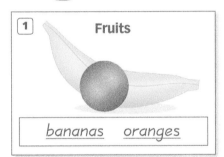

1 Fruits

bananas   oranges

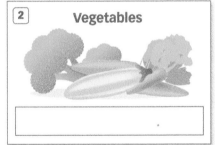

2 Vegetables

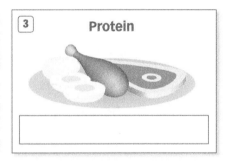

3 Protein

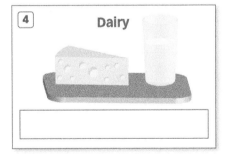

4 Dairy

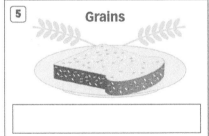

5 Grains

6 Other: Spices, Herbs, and Drinks

4 **WHAT ABOUT YOU?** Think about food you have in your kitchen. Complete the sentences.

1. I have a _____.
2. I have several _____.
3. I have a little bit of _____.
4. I have a couple of _____.
5. I have a lot of _____.
6. I have some _____.

TALK. Read your sentences to a partner.

LESSON 2: Grammar Practice Plus

 1 **LISTEN** and repeat.

1	
a box of	cereal
	crackers
	pasta

2	
a can of	soup
	tuna
	beans

3	
a bag of	rice
	chips

4	
a jar of	peanut butter
	jam
	mustard

5	
a bottle of	oil
	ketchup

6	
a carton of	milk
	juice

7	
a bunch of	bananas
	grapes

8	
a loaf	of bread

2 **CIRCLE** the correct container.

1. We need a (box)/ **jar** of cereal.
2. I bought a **jar** / **carton** of milk.
3. She ate a **loaf** / **bunch** of grapes.
4. There are three **cans** / **cartons** of soup.
5. We bought three **bags** / **bottles** of rice.
6. I have a **jar** / **bottle** of olive oil.

Math: Calculate Prices

Complete the chart. Compare the cost of Milk A, Milk B, Milk C.
Then circle the milk that is the cheapest per quart.

Item	Number of Quarts	Total Price	Price per Quart $ total price ÷ quarts =			
Milk A	4	$ 6.00	$ 6.00	÷	4	= $ 1.50
Milk B		$	$	÷		= $
Milk C		$	$	÷		= $

Read the math: $6.00 divided by 4 equals $1.50.

3 TALK with a partner. Who bought the food? What did the person buy? How do the parents feel?

4 LISTEN to the sentences. Circle *True* or *False*.

1. True   False
2. True   False
3. True   False
4. True   False
5. True   False
6. True   False

5 TALK. Work with a partner. Ask questions about what Pedro bought.

Did Pedro buy milk?

Yes, he bought five cartons of milk.

Did Pedro buy spinach?

No, he didn't.

6 WRITE sentences about the picture.

1. *Pedro bought five cartons of milk.*

2. _____

3. _____

4. _____

LESSON 3: Listening and Conversation

Pronunciation: *I like* and *I'd like*

> **I'd like** and **I would like** are polite ways to say **I want**. We often use **I'd like** when we order food in a restaurant.

A **LISTEN** and repeat the sentences.

TCD3, 20
SCD, 41

like	**'d like**
1. I like bananas.	I'd like a banana.
2. She likes cereal.	She'd like cereal.
3. We like yogurt.	We'd like yogurt.
4. They like chicken.	They'd like chicken.

B **LISTEN** to the sentences. Circle the words you hear.

TCD3, 21
SCD, 42

1. **I like / I'd like** steak.
2. **We like / We'd like** soup.
3. **They like / They 'd like** sandwiches.
4. **I like / I'd like** to go to that restaurant.
5. **We like / We'd like** chicken for dinner.
6. **I like / I'd like** that cake.

1 **LISTEN** to the question. Then listen to the conversation. Fill in the correct answer.

TCD3, 22

1. Ⓐ Ⓑ Ⓒ   2. Ⓐ Ⓑ Ⓒ   3. Ⓐ Ⓑ Ⓒ   4. Ⓐ Ⓑ Ⓒ

2 **LISTEN.** Circle the items Marta orders.

TCD3, 23

Liza's

Soups and Salads		
Onion Soup	cup 4.00	bowl 6.50
Vegetable Soup	cup 4.25	bowl 7.00
Chicken Soup	cup 5.00	bowl 7.50
Green Salad		4.50

Sandwiches	
Chicken Sandwich	6.75
Tuna Sandwich	9.75
Steak Sandwich	12.00
Hamburger	7.50
Cheeseburger	7.75

Rice Dishes	
Rice with Vegetables	8.50
Rice with Chicken	9.50
Rice with Beef	10.50

Sides	
French Fries	4.75
Mixed Vegetables	3.25
Broccoli	2.50

Desserts	
Chocolate Cake	4.50
Ice Cream (Chocolate or Vanilla)	3.50
Fruit Bowl	3.00

Beverages	
Iced Tea	1.50
Soda (Cola, Lemon–Lime, Orange)	1.70
Tea	2.00
Coffee	2.50
Milk	2.25

3 **LISTEN** and read.

A: Are you ready to order?

B: Yes, I am.

A: Would you like to start with some soup or salad?

B: Yes. I'd like a green salad.

A: What would you like for your main course?

B: I'd like a chicken sandwich.

A: Okay. Would you like something to drink?

B: Yes. I'd like some iced tea, please.

A: Would you like anything else?

TCD3, 25

LISTEN AGAIN and repeat. Then practice with a partner.

4 **PRACTICE THE CONVERSATION** with a partner.

1 some onion soup/a steak sandwich/
some coffee/some chocolate ice cream

3 some vegetable soup/rice with chicken and
mixed vegetables/a glass of lemonade/
a fruit bowl

2 a green salad/a tuna sandwich and French
fries/some iced tea/some chocolate cake

4 some chicken soup/rice with beef and broccoli/
a cup of hot tea/some vanilla ice cream

5 **TALK.** Take food orders from two classmates and complete the chart below. Use the menu in
Activity 2. Then add up the total of each person's order.

Name Mika		Name		Name	
green salad	$4.50	_____	$ _____	_____	$ _____
chicken sandwich	$6.75	_____	$ _____	_____	$ _____
iced tea	$1.50	_____	$ _____	_____	$ _____
fruit bowl	$3.00	_____	$ _____	_____	$ _____
TOTAL	$ _____	TOTAL	$ _____	TOTAL	$ _____

LESSON 4: Grammar and Vocabulary

TCD3, 26
SCD, 44

1 **GRAMMAR PICTURE DICTIONARY.** Listen and repeat.

1
A: How <u>many</u> **servings** are in this can of soup?
B: There are two servings.

2
A: How many **ingredients** are in the soup?
B: There aren't many ingredients. The soup has four ingredients: water, beef, vegetables, and salt.

3
A: How many **calories** are in one serving?
B: There aren't many calories. There are only 150 calories in one serving.

4
A: How much **protein** is in the soup?
B: There's a lot of protein. There are 20 **grams** of protein.

5
A: Is there any **iron** in the soup?
B: Yes, there is a little bit of iron.

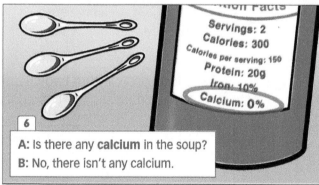

6
A: Is there any **calcium** in the soup?
B: No, there isn't any calcium.

Calories: Most people eat about 1,800 to 2,500 calories a day. You need calories for energy. But too many calories can make you gain weight.

Protein: You can get protein from foods like beef, chicken, fish, eggs, nuts, and beans.

Gram: A metric unit of measurement for a very small amount.

Iron: Iron is important for health. You can get really tired if you don't eat iron. You can get iron from meat and fish.

Calcium: There is a lot of calcium in milk. It's good for your bones and teeth. Dairy products have a lot of calcium.

 2 **NOTICE THE GRAMMAR.** Look at Activity 1. <u>Underline</u> *much*, *many*, and *any*.

Questions and Statements with Count Nouns and Non-Count Nouns

Affirmative Statements

count	There are	**many**	calories in the cookies.
non-count	There is	**some**	calcium in the cookies.

Negative Statements

count	There aren't	**any**	vitamins in the cookies.
non-count	There isn't	**any**	iron in the cookies.

Questions

| count | Are there | **any** | vitamins in the cookies? |
	Are there	**many**	calories?
non-count	Is there	**any**	iron in the cookies?
	Is there	**much**	calcium?

3 READ. Circle the correct choices.

1. *A:* Is there **any** / **many** chicken in this soup?

   B: Yes, there is **a little bit of** / **many** chicken.

2. *A:* Is there **a lot of** / **many** salt in this rice?

   B: No, there isn't **much** / **many** salt in the rice.

3. *A:* How **much** / **many** calories are in a serving of this soup?

   B: There aren't **much** / **many** calories in a serving. A serving is only 30 calories.

4. *A:* Is there **any** / **many** calcium in this milk?

   B: Yes! There is **many** / **a lot of** calcium in the milk. Milk is very good for you!

4 WHAT ABOUT YOU? Complete the sentences. Write about the food you ate and the beverages you drank yesterday. Then share your sentences with a partner.

1. I ate a lot of _____ yesterday.

2. I ate a few _____ yesterday.

3. I didn't eat any _____ yesterday.

4. I drank a lot of _____ yesterday.

5. I drank a little _____ yesterday.

6. I didn't drink any _____ yesterday.

LESSON 5: Grammar Practice Plus

1 **READ** the paragraph. Find the boldfaced words from the nutrition label in the paragraph. (Circle) them.

Nutrition facts labels can help you choose healthy food for your family. Don't buy food with a lot of fat or sodium. Too much fat can be bad for your heart. It can make you gain weight. Sodium is another word for salt. You should not eat more than 2,400 milligrams (2.4 grams) of sodium each day. Vitamins help us stay healthy. You need many different kinds of vitamins each day. Also, read the ingredients. Many foods have a lot of sugar. Sugar is not good for you and can make you gain weight.

Ana's Chunky Salsa

Nutrition Facts
Serving Size: 2 tbsp   Servings: 14

Calories	10
Total Fat	0g
Sodium	105mg
Protein	0g
Vitamin A	4%
Vitamin C	0%
Calcium	0%
Iron	0%

Ingredients: tomatoes, water, chili peppers, bell peppers, onions, vinegar, salt, sugar, garlic, pepper

2 **WRITE** each word in the chart.

sodium	~~protein~~	fat	iron	sugar	calcium	vitamins

Good for You	Not Good for You
protein	

3 **READ** the nutrition label in Activity 1. Complete the questions. Then write answers.

1. How _____*many*_____ calories are in each serving of salsa?

   There are 10 calories in each serving of salsa.

2. How _____ sodium per serving is in the salsa?

   _____

3. How _____ fat is there?

   _____

4. How _____ ingredients are there?

   _____

4 **READ** the nutrition labels for two cans of soup. Complete the question. Write the answers.

A | Mitchell's Chicken Noodle Soup

Nutrition Facts

Serving Size: 1 cup   Servings: 2

Calories	160
Total Fat	5g
Sodium	2200mg
Protein	8g
Vitamin A	14%
Vitamin C	0%
Calcium	3%
Iron	10%

Ingredients: water, onions, carrots, chicken, salt, garlic, pepper

B | Laurie's Chicken Noodle Soup

Nutrition Facts

Serving Size: 1 cup   Servings: 2

Calories	120
Total Fat	2g
Sodium	400mg
Protein	14g
Vitamin A	20%
Vitamin C	3%
Calcium	5%
Iron	14%

Ingredients: chicken, carrots, tomatoes, onions, water, garlic, salt, pepper

1. (fat) How _____much fat per serving is_____ in Soup A? ___5 grams___ Soup B? ___2 grams___

2. (calories) How _____ in Soup A? _____ Soup B? _____

3. (sodium) How _____ in Soup A? _____ Soup B? _____

4. (protein) How _____ in Soup A? _____ Soup B? _____

TALK. Discuss the question with a partner.

Which soup is better for you? Why?

5 **WRITE.** Look at the pictures. Write each food and drink in the correct place in the correct column. Then write three more items to each column.

Good for You	Not Good for You
	potato chips

CIRCLE the things that you eat or drink often.

LESSON 6: Apply Your Knowledge

1 **READ** about everything Minh ate and drank yesterday.

breakfast	1 cup of rice, 1 cup of orange juice, 2 cups of tea
lunch	1 sandwich (2 slices of bread, 1 small can tuna), 1 salad (1 cup lettuce, 1 cup tomatoes), 1 glass of cola
snacks at school	1 orange
dinner	1 cup rice, 2 cups vegetables, 1 small steak, 1 cup milk
snacks at home	1 cup of yogurt

2 **READ** the chart below. Then complete the chart with information about what Minh ate yesterday.

	Every day, we should eat …	Number of servings Minh ate yesterday
Grains	**6–7 servings** 1 serving = 1 slice of bread, 5 crackers, 1 cup of cereal, ½ cup of cooked rice or pasta, 1 small tortilla	6
Vegetables	**2–3 servings** 1 serving = 1 cup of any fresh vegetable	
Fruit	**2–3 servings** 1 serving = 1 small apple or orange, 1 cup of any fresh fruit juice	
Dairy	**3 servings** 1 serving = 1 cup of milk, 1 cup of yogurt, 2 slices of cheese	
Protein	**2 servings** 1 serving = 1 small hamburger, 1 small steak (the size of a deck of cards), ½ chicken breast, 1 small can of tuna, 1 cup of beans, 1 egg	

3 **WHAT ABOUT YOU?** Complete the sentences.

1. I should eat more _____

2. I should eat less _____

3. I eat the right amount of _____

4 LISTEN and read.

TCD3, 27
SCD, 45

A: What did you have for breakfast today?

B: Well, I had some donuts and some coffee.

A: How many donuts did you eat?

B: I ate two donuts.

A: How much coffee did you drink?

B: I drank about four cups.

5 PRACTICE THE CONVERSATION with a partner.

| 1 | 2 | 3 |

breakfast

breakfast

breakfast

| 4 | 5 | 6 |

lunch

lunch

lunch

TALK with a partner. Which meals are healthy? Which ones are not healthy?

6 WHAT ABOUT YOU? Make a plan for your meals tomorrow. Then read your plan to a partner.

Breakfast	*1 cup of cereal with strawberries, 1 cup of orange juice, 1 cup of tea*
Lunch	
Dinner	
Snacks	

LESSON 7: Reading

1 THINK ABOUT IT. Do you like to cook or bake? Do you sometimes use a recipe? What do you like to make?

> **Reading Tip**
>
> When you read **instructions** about how to do something or make something, read *all* of the instructions before you start.

2 BEFORE YOU READ. Look at the recipe and answer the questions.

1. How many ingredients are in the recipe? _____

2. How many steps are there in the recipe? _____

3 READ the recipe. Check ☑ the ingredients you have in your kitchen.

Spaghetti with Meat Sauce (8 servings)

1 box spaghetti (cooked)	2 cups of chopped carrots
3 tablespoons olive oil	1-1/2 pounds ground beef
1 onion, chopped	1 large can chopped tomatoes
3 cloves garlic, chopped	salt and pepper

1. First, put the olive oil in a pan. When the oil is hot, add the chopped onions, garlic, and carrots. Cook the onions and garlic for 5 minutes.
2. Next, add the ground beef and cook for 10 minutes.
3. Then add the chopped tomatoes, and a little salt and pepper.
4. Turn the heat to low and cook the sauce for 25 minutes.
5. Finally, put the cooked spaghetti on a plate and pour the sauce over it.

4 WRITE. Answer the questions.

1. Is there any protein in this recipe? _Yes, there is._____

2. Is there any dairy in this recipe? _____

3. Are there any vegetables in this recipe? _____

4. Are there any grains in this recipe? _____

5 TALK with a partner. Do you think this is a healthy recipe? Why or why not?

Writing

1 **BEFORE YOU WRITE.** What recipe do you know?
What food do you know how to make?

_____

Writing Tip

For a recipe, use **imperative** sentences: **Chop** the onions. **Cook** the onions.

2 **WRITE.** List the ingredients and the amounts.

Amount	Ingredient
_____	_____
_____	_____
_____	_____
_____	_____
_____	_____

3 **WRITE** directions. Explain how to make your recipe.

1. _____

_____

2. _____

_____

3. _____

_____

4. _____

_____

5. _____

_____

4 **CHECK** ☑ the directions for your recipe. Did you write about every ingredient?
Did you write every step?

5 **TALK.** Read your recipe to your partner.

1 READ AND LISTEN. Then practice with a partner.

Hmmm. I eat salads every day but I don't lose weight. Maybe some of this food has a lot of calories.

Hello Oscar. Chef Alfonso wants to plan a new menu. I would like to get some ideas for some new salads.

That's great, Lena. I have some suggestions!

Let's see: Marvin suggested potato salad with deli meat and cheese. Eric suggested we serve Italian bread with the salad. What do you think, Oscar?

We should serve healthier food. How about a spinach salad with tomatoes?

You're right, Oscar. And Chef Alfonso really wants a healthier menu!

2 TALK with a partner. Answer the questions.

1. Who wants to change the menu?

2. What salad does Marvin suggest?

3. What does Eric want to serve with the salad?

4. What does Oscar suggest?

3 WHAT ABOUT YOU? Do you eat healthy food? Do you sometimes eat food that has a lot of calories, fat, or sodium? What foods are healthy for a salad menu?

Check Your Progress!

Skill	Circle the correct words.	Is it correct?
A. Talk about amounts with count and non-count nouns.	1. I have **a few** / **a little** rice. 2. I bought **some** / **a little** carrots. 3. I have **a lot** / **a lot of** chicken in my refrigerator. 4. I'd like **a few** / **some** coffee.	☐ ☐ ☐ ☐

| | | Number Correct | 0 | 1 | 2 | 3 | 4 |

Skill	Circle the correct words.	Is it correct?
B. Ask questions about amounts with count and non-count nouns.	5. How **much** / **many** servings are in this can of soup? 6. How **much** / **many** calories are in one serving? 7. Is there **a lot of** / **many** salt in the soup? 8. Is there **any** / **many** chicken in the soup?	☐ ☐ ☐ ☐

| | | Number Correct | 0 | 1 | 2 | 3 | 4 |

Skill	Circle the correct words.	Is it correct?
C. Talk about nutrition.	9. Beef is a **protein** / **grain**. 10. An apple is a **vegetable** / **fruit**. 11. Yogurt is a **fruit** / **dairy**. 12. Rice is a **protein** / **grain**.	☐ ☐ ☐ ☐

| | | Number Correct | 0 | 1 | 2 | 3 | 4 |

Skill	Circle the correct words.	Is it correct?
D. Plan a healthy meal.	13. A healthy breakfast is **donut and coffee** / **orange juice and cereal**. 14. A healthy lunch is **salad and soup** / **hot dog and French fries**. 15. A healthy dinner is **a large hamburger** / **rice, fish, green beans**. 16. A healthy snack is **an apple** / **ice cream**.	☐ ☐ ☐ ☐

| | | Number Correct | 0 | 1 | 2 | 3 | 4 |

COUNT the number of correct answers above. Fill in the circles.

Chart Your Success					
Skill	Needs Practice	Needs Practice	Okay	Very Good	Excellent!
A. Talk about amounts with count and non-count nouns.	⓪	①	②	③	④
B. Ask questions about amounts with count and non-count nouns.	⓪	①	②	③	④
C. Talk about nutrition.	⓪	①	②	③	④
D. Plan a healthy meal.	⓪	①	②	③	④

LESSON 9: Grammar and Vocabulary

1 GRAMMAR PICTURE DICTIONARY Listen and repeat.

TCD3, 29
SCD, 46

1
Elm Street is **busy**.

2
Pine Street is **busier** than Elm Street.

3
Maple Street is **the busiest** street in the neighborhood.

4
Cherry Street is **the quietest** street in the neighborhood.

5
This is **the most expensive** supermarket in the neighborhood.

6
This is **the cheapest** supermarket in the neighborhood.

7
This is **the most dangerous** intersection in town.

8
This is **the safest** intersection in town.

9
This is **the closest** school to my house.

2 NOTICE THE GRAMMAR. Look at Activity 1. Underline the adjectives that end in -*est*. Circle the adjectives that come after the word *most*.

Superlative Adjectives

We use superlative adjectives to compare three or more people, places, or things.

Adjective	Comparative Adjective	Superlative Adjective
Eve's house is **large**.	Tim's house is **larger than** Eve's house.	Alan's house is **the largest** of the three houses.

Rules	Examples
Add *-est* or *-st* to most **one-syllable adjectives**.	the old**est** the safe**st**
For **one-syllable adjectives ending in consonant + vowel + consonant**, double the consonant and add *-est*.	the big**gest** the thin**nest**
For **two-syllable adjectives ending in -y**, change the *-y* to *i* and add *-est*.	busy ⟶ bus**iest** noisy ⟶ nois**iest**
For adjectives with **two or more syllables that do *not* end in -y**, use the words *the most*.	**the most** expensive **the most** dangerous
Some adjectives have **irregular** superlative forms.	good ⟶ **the best** bad ⟶ **the worst**

3 **WRITE.** Complete each sentence with the superlative form of an adjective from Activity 1.

1. Bob's is _____*the cheapest*_____ gas station in town. The gas is not expensive.

2. Miller Park is _____ park to my home. I can walk to the park in five minutes.

3. The intersection at Main Street and Market Street is _____ intersection in town. There are many accidents on that street each week.

4. South Street is _____ street in the city. There are always a lot of cars and people crossing the street there.

5. Green's Market is _____ supermarket in town. The food costs a lot.

4 **WHAT ABOUT YOU?** Ask and answer the questions with a partner.

1. What is the quietest street near your school?

2. What is the busiest street near your school?

3. What is the closest supermarket to your school?

4. What is the biggest park near your school?

LESSON 2: Grammar Practice Plus

1 WRITE. Look at the ads. Write the abbreviations next to the words.

1. apartment _____apt._____
2. bathroom _____
3. bedroom _____
4. dining room _____
5. furnished _____

6. unfurnished _____
7. garage _____
8. kitchen _____
9. large _____
10. living room _____

11. per month _____
12. small _____
13. washer and dryer _____

A
2 br apt. Sm kit, lr, no gar. **W/D, unfurn. No pets.** **$550/mo.**

B
Beautiful 3 br 3 ba apt! Lg kit, lr, dr, lg gar, W/D unfurn. Pets OK. $950/mo.

C
Nice 1 br 1 ba apt. Furn, lg kit, sm lr, W/D. No pets. $775/mo.

2 WRITE. Lucy is looking for a new apartment. Read the ads in Activity 1. Then answer the questions.

1. Which apartment has furniture? _____Apartment C_____

2. Which apartment has a garage? _____

3. Which apartment is the most expensive? _____

4. Which apartment is the cheapest? _____

5. Which apartment is the largest? _____

6. Which apartment is the smallest? _____

Math: Calculate money for rent

Math lesson: What is 25% of $100? To find the answer, follow these steps.
1. Change the percent to a decimal: 25% = .25
2. Multiply the decimal times the number: .25 × 100 = $25

A CIRCLE the answers.

1. What is 30% of 100?   45   30   25
2. What is 40% of 200?   80   40   160

3. What is 10% of 500?   10   50   70
4. What is 25% of 400?   25   250   100

B CALCULATE the amount of money Bill can spend for rent.

Bill earns $1,200 each month. He is planning to spend 30% of his salary for rent. How much can he spend for rent ? $_____

3 **TALK** about the pictures.

Apartment building 1

Apartment building 2

BUILT 1987

2 br apt.
$1000 month

Apartment building 3

BUILT 2005

2 br apt.
$1300 month

2 br apt.
$1100 month

BUILT 1965

> Apartment building 1 is in a busy neighborhood.

4 **WRITE.** Complete the sentences about the pictures.

1. Apartment building _____1_____ is on the busiest street.

2. Apartment building _____ is on the quietest street.

3. The rent in apartment building _____ is the most expensive.

4. Apartment building _____ is the newest building.

5. The rent in apartment building _____ is the cheapest.

6. Apartment building _____ is the oldest.

5 **TALK.** Write four true or false statements about the apartments. Read the sentences to a partner. Your partner says *That's true* or *That's false*.

> Apartment building 1 is the smallest.

> That's false!

> That's true!

> Apartment building 1 is the newest.

LESSON 3: Listening and Conversation

TCD3, 30

1 **LISTEN** to the question. Then listen to the conversation. Fill in the correct answer.

1. Ⓐ　　Ⓑ　　Ⓒ

2. Ⓐ　　Ⓑ　　Ⓒ

3. Ⓐ　　Ⓑ　　Ⓒ

4. Ⓐ　　Ⓑ　　Ⓒ

5. Ⓐ　　Ⓑ　　Ⓒ

6. Ⓐ　　Ⓑ　　Ⓒ

TCD3, 31

LISTEN AGAIN. Complete the chart with information from the conversations and the ads.

	Apartment A	Apartment B	Apartment C
Number of Bedrooms	2		
Furnished?			
Garage?			
Pets OK?			
Washer/Dryer?			

2 **WRITE** the number of each apartment under the correct ad.

A
1 br apt, 2 ba, lg lr, nice dr, lg kit, 3 lg closets, 1 sm closet in kit. No gar. No W/D. No pets. $845/mo.

Apartment _____

B
3 br apt, furn, 2 ba, nice kit, lg lr, 4 lg closets. Gar. W/D in apt. Cats OK, but no dogs. $825/mo.

Apartment _____

C
2 br apt, 1 ba, furn, lg kit, dr, nice lr. 2 lg closets. Gar. W/D. Hardwood floors. Pets OK. $660/mo.

Apartment _____

3 **WRITE.** Choose the apartment that you like best. Then complete the sentence below.

I like apartment _____ because _____

_____

_____

_____

TCD3, 32
SCD, 47

4 LISTEN and repeat.

A: Hello. I'm calling about the three-bedroom house for rent. Is it still available?

B: Yes, it is.

A: Great. Is it furnished?

B: Yes, it is.

A: Is there a garage?

B: Yes, there's a one-car garage.

A: Is there a washer and dryer?

B: No, there isn't.

A: How far is the closest supermarket?

B: It's four blocks away.

A: Are pets OK?

B: Yes, they are.

5 PRACTICE THE CONVERSATION from Activity 4 with a partner.

1
1 br apt, unfurn, 1 ba, sm lr, sm dr, lg kit, 2 lg closets, 1 sm closet in ba. No gar. No W/D. Laundromat 1 block away. Hardwood floors. Cats OK. Supermarket 2 blocks away. $725/mo.

2
Beautiful 3 br 3 ba apt! Lg kit, lr, dr, lg, gar, W/D unfurn. Pets OK. School 1 mile away. $950/mo.

3
Nice 1 br 1 ba Furn, lg kit, 1 sm lr, W/D. No Pets. $775/mo. Playground 2 blocks away. $950/mo.

4
Clean 2 br 2 ba apt! Unfurn, sm kit, lrg lr, WD in basement. Pets OK. Dog park 4 blocks away. $800/mo.

6 WHAT ABOUT YOU? Write a description of your apartment or house for a newspaper ad.

_____

_____

_____

_____

_____

LESSON 4: Grammar and Vocabulary

1 GRAMMAR PICTURE DICTIONARY. Listen and repeat.

TCD3, 33
SCD, 48

1
A: What is the best **cable company**?
B: Smith Cable is the best.

2
A: Which **phone company** do you use?
B: I use Blue Bell Telephone Company.

3
A: When does the **electric company** check the meter?
B: They check it at the end of each month.

4
A: What's the number for the **gas company**?
B: The number is 555-4756.

5
A: Which **hardware store** is the largest?
B: Build-It-Yourself is the largest hardware store.

6
A: Which **drugstore** do you like?
B: I like Lincoln's Pharmacy.

7
A: What is the biggest **department store**?
B: Mason's is the biggest department store.

8
A: When does the **furniture store** open?
B: It usually opens at 10 A.M.

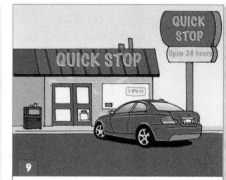

9
A: Where is the closest **convenience store**?
B: It's two blocks away.

2 NOTICE THE GRAMMAR. Look at Activity 1. Underline the questions that use a form of the verb *be*. Circle the questions that use *do* or *does* with another verb.

---

140 Use *be* and *do/does* for information.

Information Questions with *Be* and *Do*

> Use *which* when you are asking about two or more similar things.

Question Word	*be*	Adjective + Subject
Where	is	the closest bus stop?
Who	is	your plumber?
How much	are	these chairs?

Question Word	*do*	Subject	Verb
Where	does	this bus	go?
Who	does	he	need?
How much	do	these chairs	cost?

Which + Noun	*be*	Adjective
Which store	is	the best?

Which + Noun	*do*	Subject	Verb
Which store	do	you	like?

---

3 **WRITE.** Complete the questions. Then match each question to the best answer.

_c_ 1. __Where__ does he buy his clothes?

____ 2. _____ is the best time to go shopping?

____ 3. _____ drugstore do you go to?

____ 4. _____ do you buy milk?

____ 5. _____ is the best gas station?

a. In the morning.

b. The pharmacy on the corner of Pine and Lake.

c. At a department store.

d. Zippy Gas and Go.

e. At the convenience store on 1st Street.

---

4 **WHAT ABOUT YOU?** Put the words in order to make questions. Then ask and answer the questions with a partner.

1. neighborhood / in your / drugstore / What / the largest / is / ?

   What is the largest drugstore in your neighborhood?

2. you / do / grocery shopping / usually go / When / ?

   _____

3. are / department stores / the best / Which / ?

   _____

4. do / buy / at convenience stores / What / you / ?

   _____

5. in your neighborhood / the best drugstore / What / is / ?

   _____

LESSON 5: Grammar Practice Plus

1 **CIRCLE** the correct form of *be* or *do*.

1. What **does** / **is** she need?

2. When **are** / **do** you like to shop?

3. Where **is** / **does** the largest drugstore?

4. Which furniture store **does** / **do** he like?

5. What **is** / **are** the cost for cable TV?

6. Which phone companies **is** / **are** the cheapest?

TCD3, 34

2 **LISTEN** and repeat.

electrician

locksmith

exterminator

plumber

superintendent

carpenter

3 **WRITE.** Complete the questions with the words from Activity 2.

1. Who is the best _____*plumber*_____? Something is wrong with my toilet.

2. Which _____ do you call when you lose your keys?

3. Who is the cheapest _____? I have bugs in my apartment.

4. Who is the _____ of the apartment of building? I have a lot of problems with my apartment.

5. My wood table is broken. Who is a good _____?

6. Who is the best _____? The lights in my apartment don't work.

Pronunciation: *th/d*

A **LISTEN** and repeat.

TCD3, 35
SCD, 49

1. than	Dan	3. their	dare	5. then	den
2. they	day	4. lather	ladder	6. those	doze

B **LISTEN.** (Circle) the words you hear.

TCD3, 36
SCD, 50

1. than	Dan	3. their	dare	5. then	den
2. they	day	4. lather	ladder	6. those	doze

C **LISTEN** and repeat.

TCD3, 37
SCD, 51

1. There is a sale at that department store every day.
2. Their house is the largest house on this street.
3. This is the most dangerous intersection in this city.
4. This desk is bigger than that desk.

4 **READ** the paragraph. Then complete the questions. Write the question words and the correct form of *be* or *do*. Use these question words.

Why	Who	Which	What

Lucy has a lot of problems with her new apartment. Her superintendent, Mr. Santos, usually fixes small problems, but he can't fix big problems. So Lucy calls a different person to fix each problem. She calls the gas company for problems with her gas water heater. She calls Sam Barker to fix her toilet. He is a plumber. She calls an electrician to fix her lights. She calls a carpenter, Alan Chen, to fix her doors and shelves. He is the best carpenter in town.

1. *A:* ____Why____ ____does____ Lucy call the gas company?
   B: She calls the gas company because she has problems with her gas water heater.

2. *A:* _____ _____ Sam Barker?
   B: He is Lucy's plumber.

3. *A:* _____ _____ she call the plumber?
   B: She calls him because she has a problem with her toilet.

4. *A:* _____ _____ Alan Chen's job?
   B: He is a carpenter.

5. *A:* _____ _____ Alan Chen fix in Lucy's apartment?
   B: He fixes her doors and cabinets.

LESSON 6: Apply Your Knowledge

1 READ. Look at the advertisements below. Circle the cost per month and the free gifts.

ClearBell Cellular

Service starting at just

$29.95 for

3,000 minutes

GET A FREE CAMERA PHONE when you sign up!

14 locations in the Los Angeles area

vista cellular

Come to a **vista cellular** store this weekend and get a **FREE** wireless headset.

Get 4,000 minutes for $26.95 a month.

Mobile Life Cellular

We offer the best rates!

Get **3,000** minutes for just **$22.95** a month!

Sign up now and get a **FREE CELL PHONE!**

TCD3, 38

2 LISTEN to the conversation. Look at the ads in Activity 1. Which company is the person talking to? Circle your answer.

a. ClearBell Cellular

b. Vista Cellular

c. Mobile Life Cellular

TCD3, 39

3 LISTEN and complete the chart below.

	Monthly Rates	Number of Minutes	Free Gifts
1.			
2.			
3.			

Which cell phone company should Lucy choose? _____

Why? _____

Compare phone company service plans.

4 **LISTEN** and read.

TCD3, 40
SCD, 52

A: **Wolf Cable.** How may I help you?

B: Hello. I'd like to order **basic cable TV service.**

A: Okay. Let me schedule a service person. What days are good for you?

B: **Mondays and Tuesdays** are good for me.

A: How about **Monday between 10:00 and 2:00**?

B: That's fine.

TCD3, 41
LISTEN AGAIN and repeat. Then practice with a partner.

5 **PRACTICE THE CONVERSATION** with a partner.

1 Western Gas and Electric Company/
gas and electricity/
Thursdays and Fridays/
Friday between 2:00
and 5:00.

2 Mountain Bell Telephone Company/
telephone service/
Mondays and Wednesdays/
Wednesday between
8:00 A.M. and noon.

3 Link-Up Internet Service/
an Internet connection/
Tuesdays and Fridays/
Friday between 9:00 A.M.
and 3:00 P.M.

6 **PUT IT TOGETHER. Step 1:** complete the questions in the dialogue with a form of *be* or *do*. **Step 2:** Student B: Turn to page 198. Use the information there to answer Student A's questions. Then practice the dialogue together.

A: Can you suggest a good bakery?

B: Yes, _____*Cupcake Bakery*_____ is good.

A: What _____*is*_____ the address?

B: _____

A: What time _____ the bakery open in the morning?

B: _____

A: What _____ the price for a cake?

B: _____

A: How much _____ a loaf of bread?

B: _____

LESSON 7: Reading

1 THINK ABOUT IT. Do you ever fix things in your house or apartment? What do you fix?

2 BEFORE YOU READ. Read each problem. Write *R* next to each item that you think the renter needs to fix. Write *LL* next to each item that you think the landlord needs to fix.

_____ 1. There is no hot water.

_____ 2. The roof is leaking. The water is coming into our apartment.

_____ 3. The bathroom is leaking.

_____ 4. The lock on the front door of the building is broken.

_____ 5. The windows are dirty.

Reading Tip

You can use **pictures** to help you understand new words when you read.

3 READ the article. Underline the words in the article that match the pictures.

What is Your Landlord Responsible for?

Do you rent an apartment? It is important to understand your rights and responsibilities. Your landlord is responsible for making your apartment safe to live in. For example, he or she needs to fix unsafe things such as broken stairs or a broken lock. Your landlord is also responsible for making sure that your apartment is comfortable. It isn't your landlord's responsibility to give you nice furniture, but your landlord must fix broken water heaters, take care of problems with cockroaches and other bugs, and fix leaking roofs. But sometimes, renters are responsible for small problems, such as leaking faucets and broken windows. If you are not sure who is responsible for fixing a problem in your apartment, check your rental lease and the laws in your state.

4 WHAT is the main idea? Circle the main idea.

A. Landlords are responsible for fixing all the problems in the apartments.

B. Landlords are required to make your apartment safe and comfortable.

C. Landlords have responsibilities for problems and renters have some responsibilities, too.

Writing

1 **WRITE** the names of the best businesses in your town. Complete the chart below.

Business	Name of best business in my town
supermarket	
coffee shop	
drugstore	
fast food restaurant	

2 **TALK.** Vote for the best business in your town. Your teacher will write your answers to Activity 1 on the board.

3 **TALK** with a partner. Count the answers that your teacher wrote on the board. Which places have the most votes? Complete the chart below.

Type of business	Name of business with most votes	Number of Votes
supermarket		
coffee shop		
drug store		
fast food restaurant		

4 **WRITE** sentences about the best businesses in your town. Use the information in Activity 3.

1. The best supermarket is _____

2. _____

3. _____

4. _____

Think of two other kinds of businesses in your town. Tell a partner about the best businesses.

Career Connection

1 **READ AND LISTEN.** Then practice with a partner.

Hey Oscar, what's up?

Oh hi, Sofia. I'm finally taking a break. I called about two apartments for rent, but they weren't available.

1

What are you looking for? Maybe I can help.

Great. My wife and I need a bigger place, closer to the college. We're looking for a two-bedroom with a washer and dryer.

2

You should call my real estate agent. He helped me find a two-bedroom apartment with the best view in the neighborhood.

3

No problem, Oscar! Just call that number and ask for Boris. He's a very good agent.

Thank you so much, Sofia, this is really helpful.

4

2 **TALK** with a partner. Answer the questions.

1. What kind of apartment does Oscar want?
2. What kind of apartment does Sofia have?
3. Does Sofia help Oscar?
4. How does Sofia help?

3 **WHAT ABOUT YOU?** What do you like about your apartment or house? What don't you like? Write your answers in the chart.

Like	Don't Like

4 **ROLE-PLAY.** You are looking for a new apartment. Your partner is the real estate agent. Tell your partner the kind of apartment you are looking for. Then change roles.

Check Your Progress!

Skill	Circle the correct words.	Is it correct?
A. Compare three or more places in the community.	1. Maple Street is **the busiest**/**the busier** street in the neighborhood. 2. Bob's Fast Food has **least expensive**/**the least expensive** hamburgers in this neighborhood. 3. Lincoln Elementary is **the close**/**the closest** school to my home. 4. Mario's Restaurant is **more expensive**/**the most expensive** than Sally's Diner.	☐ ☐ ☐ ☐

		Number Correct	0	1	2	3	4

Skill	Circle the correct words.	Is it correct?
B. Ask questions about stores and services.	5. When **is**/**does** the gas company check the meter? 6. **Where**/**Which** hardware store **is**/**does** the cheapest? 7. Where **do**/**are** you shop for food? 8. What time **do**/**does** the supermarket open?	☐ ☐ ☐ ☐

		Number Correct	0	1	2	3	4

Skill	Circle the correct words.	Is it correct?
C. Read ads about apartments and houses for rent.	9. There is an apartment for rent. **A for Rent**/**Apt for Rent** 10. The apartment has furniture. **Furn.**/**Unfurn.** 11. There are three bedrooms. **3 br**/**3 ba** 12. The rent is $900 each month. **$900/mo**/**$900/yr**	☐ ☐ ☐ ☐

		Number Correct	0	1	2	3	4

Skill	Circle the correct words.	Is it correct?
D. Find services for the home.	13. My toilet is leaking. Who is the best **plumber**/**electrician**? 14. I lost my keys. Which **carpenter**/**locksmith** is the cheapest. 15. I have bugs in my new home. Which **superintendent**/**exterminator** is the best? 16. Something is wrong with my T.V. service. I need to call the **exterminator**/**cable company**.	☐ ☐ ☐ ☐

		Number Correct	0	1	2	3	4

COUNT the number of correct answers above. Fill in the bubbles.

Chart Your Success					
Skill	Needs Practice	Needs Practice	Okay	Very Good	Excellent!
A. Compare three or more places in the community.	⓪	①	②	③	④
B. Ask questions about stores and services.	⓪	①	②	③	④
C. Read ads about apartments and houses for rent.	⓪	①	②	③	④
D. Find services for the home.	⓪	①	②	③	④

LESSON 1: Grammar and Vocabulary

1 GRAMMAR PICTURE DICTIONARY. Listen and repeat.

TCD4, 2
SCD, 53

DEPT. OF MOTOR VEHICLES

1 INFORMATION

I want to get a **driver's license**. What do I have to do?

2 INFORMATION

First, you have to fill out an **application**.

APPLICATION

3 DRIVING TEST

Then you have to pay the **fee**. It's $30.00.

4

Next you have to take the **written test**.

5

You passed your test. Here's your **learner's permit**.

6

I have to **practice driving**.

DMV

7

Then I have to take my **driving test**.

CALIFORNIA DRIVERS LICENSE

EXPIRES 02·24·08

8

His license **expired** last week.

DEPT. OF MOTOR VEHICLES

9

He has to **renew** his license.

2 NOTICE THE GRAMMAR. Look at Activity 1. Underline *have to* and *don't have* to. Circle the verbs after *have to*.

Have to and Must

We usually say **have to**.
We rarely say **must**.

We use *have to* + verb and *must* + verb to say that something is necessary.

Affirmative

We usually use *have to* when we speak.

Subject	have to/has to	
I You We They	have to	take the driving test.
He She	has to	

Negative

Don't have to means something isn't necessary.

Subject	don't have to/ doesn't have to	
I You We They	don't have to	take the driving test.
He She	doesn't have to	

Affirmative

We usually use *must* to talk about rules and laws.

Subject	must	
I You He She We You They	must	wear a seatbelt.

Negative

Must not means it's important NOT to do something.

Subject	must not (musn't)	
I You He She We You They	must not (mustn't)	drive too fast.

---

3 **WRITE.** Complete the sentences with *have to* or *has to*.

1. You _____*have to*_____ take a driving test.

2. She _____ fill out an application.

3. They _____ make an appointment.

4. I _____ wash my clothes.

5. He _____ buy food.

6. We _____ study for the test.

 4 **WHAT ABOUT YOU?** Write three things you have to do this week.

1. _____

2. _____

3. _____

TALK. Read your sentences to a partner.

LESSON 2: Grammar Practice Plus

1 LISTEN and repeat.

1. stop sign	3. traffic light	5. pedestrian crosswalk	7. speed limit signs
2. turning lane	4. traffic ticket	6. yield sign	

2 MATCH to make sentences about people in the picture.

_e_	1. David has to	a.	turn left.
____	2. Mike has to	b.	wait for the traffic light arrow to turn green.
____	3. Binh and Anh have to	c.	pay for the traffic ticket.
____	4. Tina has to	d.	stop at the stop sign.
____	5. Bill has to	e.	~~walk in the pedestrian crosswalk.~~
____	6. All the drivers have to	f.	obey the speed limit.
____	7. Kim has to	g.	wait for cars to go first.

3 TALK with a partner. Ask and answer questions.

A: What does Mike have to do?

B: He has to wait for the traffic light to turn green.

4 WRITE. Complete the sentences with *has to*, *have to*, *don't have to*, or *doesn't have to*.

1. Marilyn and Tom want to get driver's licenses. They _____*have to*_____ fill out applications.

2. Mike is at a traffic light. The light is red. He _____ wait for the light to turn green.

3. You _____ buy a car before you take your driving test. You can use a friend's car for the test.

4. Bob has to renew his license, but he _____ take the driving test again. He only _____ pay a $12 fee.

5. I just passed my written test. Now, I _____ make an appointment for the driving test.

6. The speed limit sign says 65 miles per hour. You _____ drive 65 miles per hour. You can drive 55 miles per hour.

5 READ the rules below. Complete each rule with *must* or *must not*.

1. Left turn only. Drivers _____*must not*_____ turn right.

2. Everyone _____ wear a seat belt in this state. It's the law.

3. You _____ make an appointment for the driving test.

4. Drivers _____ follow all laws and safety rules.

5. People _____ bring knives or scissors on the airplane.

6. You _____ fill out an application for a driver's license. You can pick up an application at Window 14.

7. The speed limit is 35 miles an hour on this street. You _____ drive 65.

6 WRITE. Complete the sentences with *don't have to*, *doesn't have to*, or *mustn't*.

1 You _____*don't have to*_____ call me tonight. You can call me tomorrow.

2. They _____ study tonight. They are on vacation.

3. Children under six years old _____ sit in the front seat of the car. It's not safe.

4. Mark _____ work today. His office is closed for Labor Day.

5. The sign says "no parking." You _____ park there.

6. The students _____ smoke in the classroom.

7. Mike and Sue _____ shop for food today. They have a lot of food in their refrigerator.

8. My driving test is at 10:00. I _____ be late.

LESSON 3: Listening and Conversation

 1 LISTEN to the question. Then listen to the conversation. Fill in the correct answer.

1. Ⓐ Ⓑ Ⓒ   3. Ⓐ Ⓑ Ⓒ

2. Ⓐ Ⓑ Ⓒ   4. Ⓐ Ⓑ Ⓒ

 LISTEN AGAIN. Number the pictures in the correct order.

Pronunciation: *Have to (hafta), Has to (hasta)*

 A LISTEN AND REPEAT. Use careful pronunciation.

1. I have to go to the DMV after class today.

2. I have to renew my driver's license.

3. Elizabeth has to renew her driver's license, too.

4. She has to take the bus to the DMV.

5. We have to take a written test.

 B LISTEN to the relaxed pronunciation (*I hafta, He hasta*). Circle the words you hear.

1. has to / have to

2. has to / have to

3. has to / have to

4. has to / have to

5. have to / have to

| Listen and put pictures in order. • Pronunciation *have/has*.

2 **LISTEN** and read.

TCD4, 8
SCD, 56

A: Hi. Can I help you?

B: Yes, I need to **renew my driver's license**.
What do I have to do?

A: First, you have to pay the fee.

B: Do I have to **take a driving test**?

A: **No, you don't**.

B: Okay. Thank you.

 LISTEN AGAIN and repeat. Then practice with a partner.

TCD4, 9

3 **PRACTICE THE CONVERSATION** with a partner.

1 apply for a learner's permit/fill
out an application/Yes

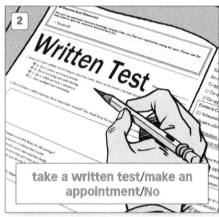

2 take a written test/make an
appointment/No

3 take a driving test/show my
learner's permit/Yes

4 **WHAT ABOUT YOU?** Write sentences about you. Use *have to* and *don't have to*.

1. learn to drive _____

2. get a driver's license _____

3. renew my driver's license _____

4. buy a car _____

5. get a job _____

TALK. Read your sentences to a partner.

I have to get a job.
I don't have to get
a driver's license.

I don't have to get a
job. I have to renew
my driver's license.

LESSON 4: Grammar Picture Dictionary

1 **GRAMMAR PICTURE DICTIONARY.** Listen and repeat.

TCD4, 10
SCD, 57

1. **Walk through** the park.

2. Go **down** Lark Street.

3. Turn **toward** the library.

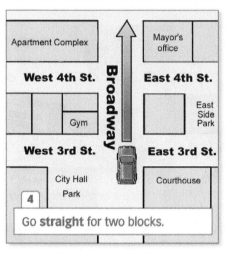
4. Go **straight** for two blocks.

5. Drive **into** the parking lot.

6. Walk **out of** the building.

7. Go **across** the street.

8. Go **north**.

9. Drive **west** on Pine Street.

2 **NOTICE THE GRAMMAR.** Look at Activity 1. Circle the verbs. Underline the words that explain directions.

Imaperatives

Imperative sentences start with the base form of a verb.

We use imperative sentences to tell people to do things (commands) and to give directions.

Affirmative Imperatives

Turn right at the traffic light and **go** toward the park.

Go through the park, and **walk** north for two blocks.

Negative Imperatives

Don't go into the parking lot.

Don't turn left.

---

3 READ. Check ☑ the sentences that use imperatives.

_____ 1. You should wear a seat belt.

_____ 2. Walk through the park and then turn right.

_____ 3. Don't drive fast!

_____ 4. They walk around the park every day.

_____ 5. Drive into that parking lot.

_____ 6. Turn right on First Street.

4 WRITE. Answer the questions. Write imperative sentences.

1. Your friend is driving too fast. What do you say?   _Don't drive fast! / Please drive carefully._

2. Your friend is turning right. The sign says LEFT TURN ONLY. What do you say?   _____

3. You are at an intersection. There is a stop sign. The driver is not stopping. What do you say?   _____

4. Your friend is driving north. You need to go south. What do you say?   _____

5 TALK with a partner. Give directions to a place near your school.

I need directions to the library.

Go down Lark Street two blocks and turn left.

LESSON 5: Grammar Practice Plus

1 **WRITE.** Complete the sentences. Use the words in the box.

around	over	past	under

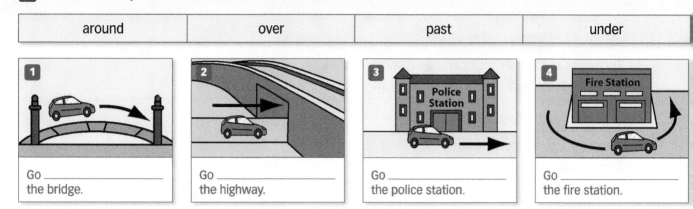

1
Go _____ the bridge.

2
Go _____ the highway.

3
Go _____ the police station.

4
Go _____ the fire station.

TCD4, 11

LISTEN and repeat. Are your answers correct?

2 **LOOK** at the map. Read the sentences. Answer the questions.

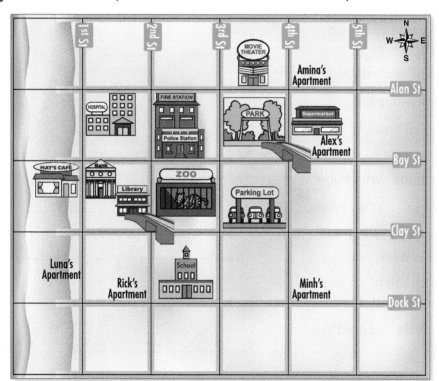

1. Start at Rick's apartment. Go north on 2nd Street. Turn right on Bay Street. Go one block. What is on your left? _____

2. Start at Amina's apartment. Go south on 4th Street. Turn right on Bay Street. Go under the bridge. Go to the next corner. What is on your left and right? _____

3. Start at Luna's apartment. Go north on 1st Street. Go past May's Café. What is on the next corner?

   _____

3 **WRITE** the directions. Use the map in Activity 2.

1. Start at the movie theater. Write directions to Minh's apartment.

   Go _____ on 4ᵗʰ Street. Go _____ the bridge. Walk

   _____ blocks. Minh's house is on the corner of _____ Street

   and _____ Street.

2. Start at Amina's apartment. Write directions to May's Café.

   Go _____ on Alan Street. Walk _____ the beach. Turn

   _____ on 1ˢᵗ Street. Walk one block. May's Café is on the _____

   of 1ˢᵗ Street and _____ Street.

3. Start at Luna's apartment. Write directions to the supermarket.

   Go _____ on 1ˢᵗ Street. Turn right. Go _____ on Clay

   Street. Go under the _____ . Walk _____ the parking garage.

   Turn _____ on 4ᵗʰ Street. Go under the _____ .

   The supermarket is on your _____ .

4 **WRITE** directions to go from Amina's apartment to Rick's apartment.

   _____

   _____

   _____

   _____

   _____

Math: Calculate Miles and Kilometers

To change miles to kilometers, multiply the number of miles by **1.6**.

Example: 10 miles × 1.6 = 16 kilometers

To change kilometers to miles, multiply the kilometers by **.62**.

Example: 10 kilometers × .62 = 6.2 miles

1. 100 miles = _____ kilometers
2. 20 miles = _____ kilometers
3. 5 miles = _____ kilometers
4. 100 kilometers = _____ miles
5. 20 kilometers = _____ miles
6. 5 kilometers = _____ miles

LESSON 6: Apply Your Knowledge

1 READ the map. Write the names of the places next to the letters on the map.

A. school	D. DMV	G. museum
B. bank	E. shoe store	H. café
C. library	F. restaurant	I. supermarket

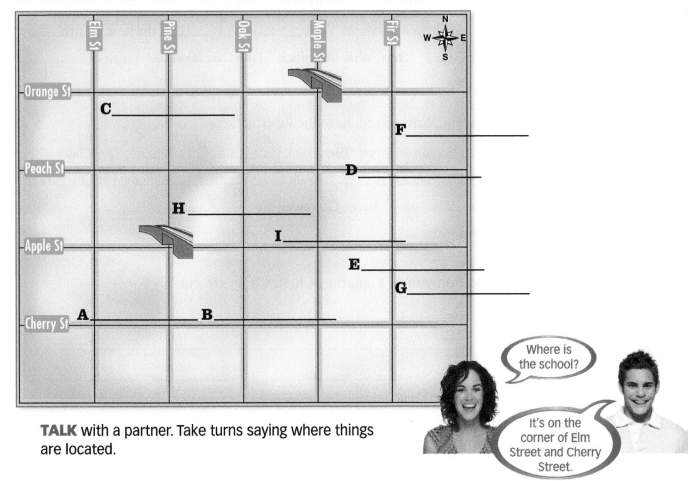

TALK with a partner. Take turns saying where things are located.

Where is the school?

It's on the corner of Elm Street and Cherry Street.

2 LISTEN. Circle the correct answer.

1. Where is Gloria going to meet her friend?

   A. Martha's Pizza   B. Maria's Cafe   C. Millie's Restaurant

2. Why is Gloria late?

   A. She's lost.   B. She has car problems.   C. She worked late.

3. Where is Gloria?

   A. in the park   B. at the supermarket   C. at the school

3 LISTEN AGAIN. Draw a line on the map above. Show the directions Carl gives to Millie.

TCD4, 13

Find places in the community. • Give, and ask for, directions.

4 **LISTEN** and read.

TCD4, 14
SCD, 58

A: Hi. I have to **renew my driver's license**. Can you give me directions from the school to **the DMV?**

B: Sure. **Go north on Elm Street and turn right on Peach Street.** It's on the right.

A: Thanks.

 LISTEN AGAIN and repeat. Practice with a partner.

TCD4, 15

5 **PRACTICE** the conversation with a partner. Use the map in Activity 1 on page 160.

1

A: shop for food / Sam's Supermarket
B: (Give directions from the school to the supermarket.)

3

A: meet a friend for a coffee
B: (Give directions from the school to Maria's Café.)

2

A: buy new shoes / Best Shoes
B: (Give directions from the school to the shoe store.)

4

A: check out book / Elm Avenue library
B: (Give directions from the school to the library.)

 6 **WHAT ABOUT YOU?** Choose a place. You and a partner write directions from your school to that place. Compare your directions with your partner's. Are they similar or different?

post office	supermarket	park	museum	restaurant

LESSON 7: Reading

1 THINK ABOUT IT. How do you usually give directions to people? By phone? By email? In person? In invitations?

2 BEFORE YOU READ. Scan the email invitation. <u>Underline</u> the names of the streets.

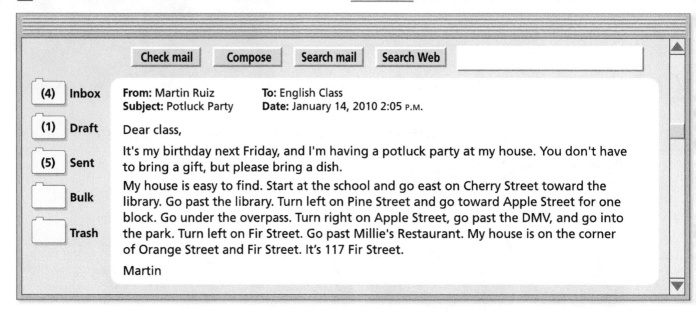

Check mail   Compose   Search mail   Search Web

(4) Inbox
(1) Draft
(5) Sent
Bulk
Trash

From: Martin Ruiz   **To:** English Class
Subject: Potluck Party   **Date:** January 14, 2010 2:05 P.M.

Dear class,

It's my birthday next Friday, and I'm having a potluck party at my house. You don't have to bring a gift, but please bring a dish.

My house is easy to find. Start at the school and go east on Cherry Street toward the library. Go past the library. Turn left on Pine Street and go toward Apple Street for one block. Go under the overpass. Turn right on Apple Street, go past the DMV, and go into the park. Turn left on Fir Street. Go past Millie's Restaurant. My house is on the corner of Orange Street and Fir Street. It's 117 Fir Street.

Martin

3 TALK. Ask a partner the questions.

1. Why is Martin having a party? _____

2. What should students bring? _____

3. How many blocks do students have to walk from the school to the Martin's house? _____

4 READ the directions in the invitation. Draw lines in the map below to show the directions from the school to the party.

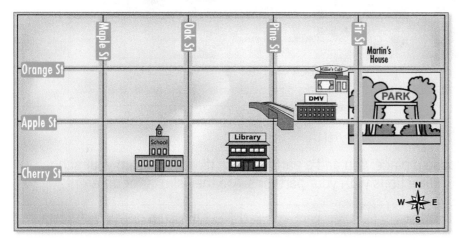

Write directions. • Create an invitation.

Writing

1 **PLAN AHEAD.** Work in a small group. Plan a party.

1. What kind of party do you want to have? (Chinese New Year party, birthday party, class party) _____

2. Where do you want to have your party? Choose a place from the map below. _____

Writing Tip

Always **edit** (check) your writing. Check your directions to make sure they are correct before you give them to someone.

2 **BEFORE YOU WRITE.** Plan the directions. Draw a line from the school to the place for the party.

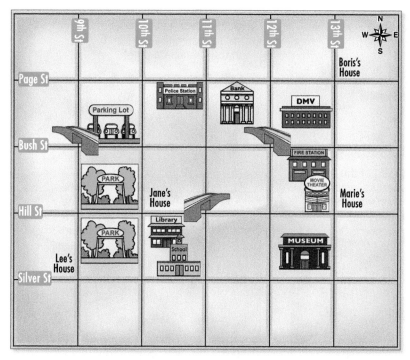

3 **WRITE** an email invitation to a party. Fill in the blanks on the invitation. Follow the example on page 162. Write directions from the school to the party.

4 **CHECK** your directions. Are they correct?

| Check mail | Compose | Search mail | Search Web | |

(4) Inbox	From: _____ To: _____
(1) Draft	Subject: _____ Date: _____
(5) Sent	Dear Friends,
Bulk	_____
Trash	_____

Career Connection

1 READ AND LISTEN. Then practice with a partner.

1

Hello. Can I help you?

Hi, uh, I'm from Champion Foods Delivery. Is Marvin here? I have to deliver some food.

2

Oh, I'm sorry. Marvin is not working today and the manager is on her break. My name is Oscar. Maybe I can help you.

I hope so. I have a lot to deliver and the chef gets upset when the food isn't in the kitchen on time!

3

Okay, I've got the list. Let's make sure everything is here. Then we can move everything into the kitchen.

Wow, thanks! Together we can do this quickly. Marvin never helps me with all this!

4

Can you tell me how to get to Ling's Chinese Restaurant?

Sure. Go straight on Third Avenue for two blocks and turn left at the light. Then go four blocks on Elm Street. The restaurant is on the left.

Thanks again!

2 TALK. Talk to a partner.

1. What does the deliveryman have to do?
2. Where is Marvin?
3. What happens when the food doesn't arrive on time?
4. What does the deliveryman want to know?

3 WHAT ABOUT YOU? How often do you shop for food? Where do you buy your food?

Talk about finding directions on the job.

Check Your Progress!

Skill	Circle the correct words.	Is it correct?
A. Make statements and questions with *have to*.	1. You **have**/**have to** pay a fee for the driver's license. 2. Tom wants to get a driver's license. What does he **have to**/**has to** do? 3. Mary and David **have to**/**has to** practice driving. 4. Maria **have**/**has to** take the written test for her driver's license.	○ ○ ○ ○

	Number Correct	0	1	2	3	4

Skill	Circle the correct words.	Is it correct?
B. Make statements with *must*, *must not*, *have to*, and *don't have to*.	5. My license is expired. I **have to**/**must not** renew it. 6. You **must**/**don't have to** wear a seat belt. 7. I **don't have to**/**must not** buy a car for my driving test. 8. The speed limit is 65 miles per hour. I **must not**/**don't have to** drive 75 miles per hour.	○ ○ ○ ○

	Number Correct	0	1	2	3	4

Skill	Circle the correct words.	Is it correct?
C. Follow road and street signs.	9. There is a **yield sign**/**traffic light**. I must wait for other cars to go first. 10. The light is red. I have to wait for the light to turn **yellow**/**green**. 11. I have to walk in the **pedestrian intersection**/**pedestrian crosswalk**. 12. The sign says "no left turn". I **must not**/**don't have to** turn left.	○ ○ ○ ○

	Number Correct	0	1	2	3	4

Skill	Circle the correct words.	Is it correct?
D. Give directions.	13. Turn **right**/**straight** on First Street. 14. Go **around**/**under** the library. The parking lot is behind the library. 15. My house is in the **front**/**middle** of the block. 16. Drive **into**/**over** the parking lot.	○ ○ ○ ○

	Number Correct	0	1	2	3	4

COUNT the number of correct answers above. Fill in the circles.

Chart Your Success					
Skill	Needs Practice	Needs Practice	Okay	Very Good	Excellent!
A. Make statements and questions with *have to*.	⓪	①	②	③	④
B. Make statements with *must*, *must not*, *have to*, and *don't have to*.	⓪	①	②	③	④
C. Follow road and street signs.	⓪	①	②	③	④
D. Give directions.	⓪	①	②	③	④

LESSON 1: Grammar and Vocabulary

1 **GRAMMAR PICTURE DICTIONARY.** Listen and repeat.

TCD4, 17
SCD, 59

1

A: What are you going to do on Friday?

B: I'm going to **go out**.

2

A: What are you going to do tonight?

B: I'm going to **study**.

3

A: Is Tom going to **stay up late** tonight?

B: Yes, he is. He's going to stay up until 2:00 A.M.

4

A: What is Tara going to do tonight?

B: She's going to **work on a project**.

5

A: Are Don and Lily going to work this weekend?

B: No, they're going to **take it easy**.

6

A: Who is Peter going to invite over for dinner?

B: He is going to **invite** Kay over for dinner.

7

A: Are they going to **go dancing** this weekend?

B: Yes, they are.

8

A: What are Martin and Lisa going to do this weekend?

B: They're going to **go hiking**.

9

A: Is Julie going to **go running** tomorrow?

B: Yes, she is.

2 **NOTICE THE GRAMMAR.** Look at Activity 1. Underline the present of *be* and *going to* in the sentences above.

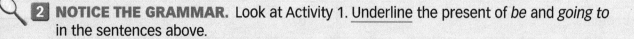

The Future with *Be Going to*

Use *be going to* to talk about future plans.

Affirmative and Negative Statements

Subject + *be*	*(not) going to*	Verb
I'm		
She's		
You're	going to not going to	study. go hiking.
We're		
They're		

You can use either form of negative contractions for the future using *be* + *going to*: He's not going to = He isn't going to.

3 **WRITE.** Complete the sentences with the correct form of *be* and *going to* or *not going to*.

1. Alan and Lucy _____*are going to*_____ invite some friends for dinner.

2. Sue _____ (not) go out tonight.

3. We _____ see a movie this weekend.

4. My brother _____ (not) visit me next month.

5. I _____ go dancing tomorrow night.

6. He _____ (not) work on his homework this afternoon.

4 **WHAT ABOUT YOU?** Walk around the classroom and talk to your classmates. Ask the questions in the chart. When classmates answer *yes*, write their names in the chart.

Are you going to . . .	Name
1. go out on Friday night?	
2. study on Friday?	
3. stay up late tomorrow night?	
4. work on a project this weekend?	
5. take it easy on Saturday?	
6. go shopping this weekend?	

5 **REPORT** your classmate's plans.

Example: Michael is going to go out on Friday night.

Are you going to go out Friday night?

Yes, I am.

LESSON 2: Grammar Practice Plus

Questions with *Be Going to*

	Yes/No Questions				Information Questions				

be	Subject	*going to*	Verb
Am	I		
Is	he		
	she	going to	study?
	you		
Are	we		
	they		

Question Word	be	Subject	*going to*	Verb
What	am	I	going to	do?
Who	is	he	going to	visit?
Where	is	she	going to	go?
When	are	you	going to	leave?
What	are	we	going to	see?
Why	are	they	going to	study?

1 **WRITE.** Complete the questions about Mark. Then write answers. Use complete sentences.

Friday night

Saturday afternoon

Sunday morning

Sunday afternoon

1. What _____*is Mark going to do*_____ (do) on Friday night?

   He's going to go to a party.

2. What _____ (do) on Saturday afternoon?

   _____

3. Where _____ (go) on Saturday afternoon?

   _____

4. Is _____ (get up early) on Sunday morning?

   _____

5. What time _____ (get up) on Sunday morning?

   _____

6. Is _____ (go hiking) on Sunday afternoon?

   _____

2 **TALK** about the picture. Say what Lucy and Lee are going to do this weekend.

3 **WRITE.** Look at the picture. Read the answers below. Write questions using *what*, *when*, *where*, or *who*.

1. *A:* Who is Lucy going to invite over for dinner on Friday night?

   B: She's going to invite Sam.

2. *A:* What _____ do on Saturday morning?

   B: She's going to go shopping.

3. *A:* Where _____ go shopping?

   B: She's going to go shopping at the mall.

4. *A:* When _____ go hiking?

   B: Lee is going to go hiking on Saturday afternoon.

4 **TALK** with a partner. Ask and answer questions about the people in the picture in Activity 2. Use *be* + *going to*.

What is Lucy going to do on Friday night?

She's going to invite Sam over for dinner.

LESSON 3: Listening and Conversation

Pronunciation: *Going to (gonna)*

 A **LISTEN** and circle the correct answer.

TCD4, 18
SCD, 60

1. *A:* Are you going to stay up late on Saturday night?
   B: **Yes, he is. / No, I'm not.**

2. *A:* Are we going to work on a project on Sunday?
   B: **Yes, we did. / Yes, we are.**

3. *A:* Is she going to go running this afternoon?
   B: **Yes, she is. / Yes, she did.**

 B **LISTEN** to the sentences. Circle *now* or *future* for each sentence.

TCD4, 19
SCD, 61

1. now   future   4. now   future

2. now   future   5. now   future

3. now   future   6. now   future

---

1 **LISTEN** to the question. Then listen to the conversation. Fill in the correct answer.

TCD4, 20

1. Ⓐ Ⓑ Ⓒ   3. Ⓐ Ⓑ Ⓒ

2. Ⓐ Ⓑ Ⓒ   4. Ⓐ Ⓑ Ⓒ

2 **LISTEN AGAIN.** Check ☑ the activities each person is going to do.

TCD4, 21

	Jill	Ed	David
1. go to the beach	☑	☐	☐
2. go shopping	☐	☐	☐
3. see a movie	☐	☐	☐
4. go hiking	☐	☐	☐
5. invite friends over for dinner	☐	☐	☐
6. relax	☐	☐	☐
7. go to a soccer game	☐	☐	☐

TALK. Tell your answers to a partner. Make sentences about Jill, Ed, and David.

Jill is going to go to the beach and . . .

3 **LISTEN** and read.

TCD4, 22
SCD, 62

A: What are you going to do this weekend?

B: I'm going to go to the beach on Saturday.

A: That sounds like fun. What about Sunday?

B: On Sunday I'm going to stay home and relax. What about you?

A: On Saturday I'm going to visit some friends.

B: Have a great weekend.

A: Thanks. You, too.

LISTEN AGAIN and repeat. Then practice with a partner.

TCD4, 23

4 **PRACTICE THE CONVERSATION** with a partner.

5 **WHAT ABOUT YOU?** Talk with your classmates. Ask and answer questions about your plans for this weekend.

What are you going to do this weekend?

I'm going to visit my family.

LESSON 4: Grammar and Vocabulary

 1 **GRAMMAR PICTURE DICTIONARY.** Listen and repeat.

TCD4, 24
SCD, 63

President's Day: February

A: What are you going to do for **President's Day**?

B: I might go to the **mountains**.

Mother's Day: May

A: What are you going to give your mother for **Mother's Day**?

B: I don't know. I might give her **flowers**.

Father's Day: June

A: Are you going to visit your dad on **Father's Day**?

B: I'm not sure. He might visit me.

Independence Day: July 4

A: Where are you going to go on **Independence Day**?

B: We might go to the beach.

Election Day: November

A: When are you and your wife going to vote on **Election Day**?

B: I don't know. We might vote in the morning.

graduate

A: When is your son going to **graduate**?

B: He might graduate next year. Or he might study for one more year.

wedding

A: Where are you going to have your **wedding**?

B: I'm not sure. We might **get married** at my parents' house.

anniversary

A: How are you going to celebrate your **anniversary** this year?

B: I don't know. We might go out to dinner.

birthday

A: What is your sister going to do for her **birthday**?

B: I'm not sure. She might have a **party**.

 2 **NOTICE THE GRAMMAR.** Look at Activity 1. Circle *might*.

Recognize American celebrations and holidays. • Use future with *may/might* and *will*.

The Future with *Might*

Use *might* to talk about future possibilities (when you are not sure).

Affirmative Statements

Subject	*might*	Verb
I You He She We You They	might	go out.

Negative Statements

Subject	*might not*	Verb
I You He She We You They	might not	go out.

3 **WRITE.** Complete the sentences with *might* and the verbs in parentheses.

1. We _____ *might get married* _____ (get married) next year.

2. I _____ (not have) a party on my birthday.

3. We _____ (go) to the beach on July 4.

4. She _____ (not go) to the mountains with us.

5. I _____ (celebrate) with my family.

6. They _____ (not go out) tomorrow night.

4 **WHAT ABOUT YOU?** Write sentences with *might* or *might not*, that are true for you.

Example: I _____ *might eat pizza for dinner* _____ tonight.

1. I _____ tonight.

2. I _____ this weekend.

3. I _____ next month.

4. I _____ next year.

5. I _____ five years from now.

6. I _____ ten years from now.

TALK. Read your sentences to a partner.

LESSON 5: Grammar Practice Plus

1 **WRITE** the words under the pictures.

| watch fireworks | get dressed up | give someone a gift | have a picnic |

_____ _____ _____ _____

LISTEN and repeat. Are your answers correct?

TCD4, 25

2 **READ** Antonio's letter to his family. Underline the plans. Circle the possibilities.

> Dear Mom and Dad,
>
> How are you? Do you know that Independence Day is on July 4 in the U.S.? My friends and I are going to have a picnic in the afternoon. We might have the picnic at the beach or we might have it at the park. Martin might come. Amina might be there, too. I'm going to make a salad for the picnic. I might make sandwiches, too.
>
> We're going to watch fireworks at the beach that night. We might stay at the beach until midnight! I'm really excited about July 4.
>
> Antonio

3 **WRITE.** Put the words in order to make questions about the letter in Activity 2.

1. going to / what holiday / Antonio / is / celebrate with his friends

   What holiday is Antonio going to celebrate with his friends?

2. going to / are / what / do / Antonio and his friends

   _____

3. be on July 4 / the weather / how / is / going to

   _____

4. are / when / leave the beach / Antonio and his friends / going to

   _____

4 **LISTEN.** Is it a plan or a possibility? Write a check ☑ next to each plan. Write a question mark (?) next to each possibility. Then write sentences with *going to* or *might*.

TCD4, 26

___✓___ **1.** Sue: go to Miami

Sue is going to go to Miami.

_____ **2.** Sue: have a party for her sister

_____

_____ **3.** Sue: make a cake

_____

_____ **4.** Sue: cook dinner

_____

_____ **5.** Alan: go to San Francisco

_____

_____ **6.** Alan: go hiking with his brother

_____

_____ **7.** Alan: visit some old friends

_____

5 **WHAT ABOUT YOU?** What is the next holiday you plan to celebrate? Ask two classmates what they are going to do for the holiday. Write their answers.

What are you going to do for Labor Day?

I might go to the beach.

Questions	Answers	
	Student 1: _____	Student 2: _____
What are you going to do?		
Who are you going to celebrate with?		
When are you going to celebrate?		
Where are you going to celebrate?		

Holiday: _____

LESSON 6: Apply Your Knowledge

🎧 **1** **LISTEN** and complete the schedule for Lucy. Add a question mark for things Lucy is not sure about.

TCD4, 27

Monday	Tuesday	Wednesday	Thursday	Friday	Saturday/ Sunday
English class	get a haircut _____ _____	English class go hiking	have lunch with _____	_____ _____ go to _____	go to _____ _____ _____

Math: Calculate Travel Time

A **READ** the paragraph about Lucy. Circle the amounts of time.

Lucy has to start work at 10:00 A.M. The bus takes 20 minutes. Then it takes Lucy eight minutes to walk from the bus stop to work. It takes her five minutes to enter the building and get to her desk. What is the latest time Lucy can catch the bus and get to work on time?

B **ADD UP** the amounts of time.

_____ min. + _____ min. + _____ min. = _____ min.

C **SUBTRACT** Lucy's travel time from the time she has to be at work.

10:00 - _____ min. = _____

Calculate travel time. • Fill out a leisure schedule.

2 **LISTEN** and read.

TCD4, 28
SCD, 64

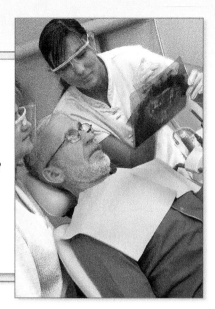

A: So, what are your plans for this week?

B: Well, I'm going to go to the dentist on Tuesday.

A: Uh-huh.

B: And I might visit my grandparents on Saturday. How about you?

A: I'm going to go to a basketball game on Wednesday night.

B: That sounds like fun.

A: On Friday night I might go to a party.

TCD4, 29 **LISTEN** and repeat. Then practice with a partner.

3 **PRACTICE THE CONVERSATION** with a partner.

1. **Plans**—work on Monday and Wednesday
   Possibilities—go hiking on Friday

   Plans—have some friends over for dinner on Tuesday
   Possibilities—go out on Friday night

2. **Plans**—work on a project on Tuesday night
   Possibilities—take it easy on Saturday and Sunday

   Plans—work on Monday through Friday
   Possibilities—go dancing on Saturday night

3. **Plans**—visit my uncle on Friday
   Possibilities—go to a party on Saturday

   Plans—study on Monday and Friday
   Possibilities—have a picnic on Saturday

4 **TALK** with a partner. In the chart write a list of three possible activities for this weekend. Make notes on the times and whom you might invite.

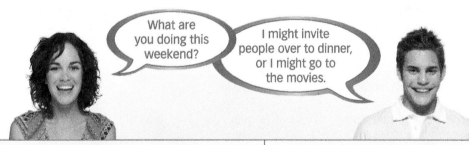

What are you doing this weekend?

I might invite people over to dinner, or I might go to the movies.

Saturday	Sunday

LESSON 7: Reading

1 **THINK ABOUT IT.** What are some activities that people do on rainy days? Think of six activities.

2 **BEFORE YOU READ.** Look at the article below. Answer the questions.

1. What city is the article about? _____

2. Who do you think is going to have fun this weekend? _____

3 **READ.** Underline the plans people have for the weekend.

Weekend Plans

DALLAS — Last weekend was warm and beautiful. But this weekend the weather is going to be very different. A big storm will come into the Dallas area on Friday that's going to last until Monday morning. I talked to a few people downtown and asked them about their plans for the weekend. Here's what they said:

Timothy W: I'm a mail carrier, so I have to work on Saturday. I'd like to take it easy and relax at home on Sunday, but my faucet is leaking and my stove doesn't work. So I'm going to stay home and repair the faucet and the stove.

Sarah M: My family and I are going to stay home all weekend. We're going to watch movies and make dinner together. I think it's going to be a great weekend!

Michael K: My friends and I are going to play football in the rain on Saturday! On Sunday, I'm going to have a party in my backyard! I love the rain!

Jan R: I'm going to write letters and call some friends. I'm also going to clean my garage and work on some projects.

4 **TALK** with a partner about the activities in the article. Answer the questions.

1. Who is going to have a fun weekend? _____

2. Who is going to work on the weekend? _____

3. Who has plans to do something outside on the weekend? _____

Writing

1 **WRITE.** Plan your weekend. In the chart list some activities you are sure you will do and some activities you might do.

Plans	Possibilities

2 **WRITE** six sentences about your plans this weekend.

Plans (use *be going to*):

1. _____

2. _____

3. _____

Possibilities (use *might*):

1. _____

2. _____

3. _____

3 **WRITE.** Write a paragraph about your plans for the weekend. Use your sentences from Activity 2.

I have some plans for this weekend. _____

_____

_____

_____

_____

_____

_____

Career Connection

1 READ AND LISTEN. Then practice with a partner.

TCD4, 30

1
It's very busy here today. Where's Marvin? It's two o'clock already!

I don't know. He's on the schedule for today from 1 P.M. to 11 P.M.

2
Marvin finally called. He isn't going to be in until 4:30, and I have to leave. Oscar, can you manage the dining room for a few hours?

Sure Lena, I can help out. No problem!

Thanks, Oscar. You sure are calm in an emergency!

3
I'm sorry Marvin, but I have to let you go. You are not responsible or serious about your job!

Uh, well, I was late because I had some car problems.

4
Marvin isn't going to work here anymore. But Chef Alfonso said that you were all a great team today. Thanks for your hard work!

2 TALK.

1. Why is Lena upset? _____

2. What did Lena ask Oscar to do today? _____

3. Why was Marvin late for work? _____

4. What did Lena do about it? _____

3 WHAT ABOUT YOU? What do you do when you are late? Does your boss get upset when you are late? How often are you late for work or for class? Does your teacher get upset when you are late for class?

Check Your Progress!

Skill	Circle the correct words.	Is it correct?				
A. Make sentences and ask questions about the future with *be going to*.	1. What are you **going do** / **going to do** this weekend? 2. Gloria and Martin **are going to** / **is going to** go hiking. 3. What **does** / **is** he going to do next Friday night? 4. I **going to** / **am going to** invite my friend to dinner.	☐ ☐ ☐ ☐				
	Number Correct	0	1	2	3	4

Skill	Circle the correct words.	Is it correct?				
B. Make sentences with *might* **and** *might not*.	5. I'm not sure about my plans. I **will** / **might** go to the beach. 6. The weather might be cold this weekend. I **might not** / **not going to** go to the beach. 7. I might stay home or I **can't** / **might** go to a movie. I'm not sure. 8. A: What is your son going to do after he graduates? B: He **might** / **might not** go to college. He is a very good student.	☐ ☐ ☐ ☐				
	Number Correct	0	1	2	3	4

Skill	Circle the correct words.	Is it correct?				
C. Talk about plans for the weekend.	9. Tom is going to go **out** / **over** tonight. He's going to see a movie. 10. I'm going to **vote** / **invite** Sam over for dinner on Saturday night. 11. I'm going to relax. I'm going to stay home and **take easy** / **take it easy**. 12. Tomorrow my friends and I are going to bring some food and eat at the park. The **picnic** / **movie** will start at 2:00.	☐ ☐ ☐ ☐				
	Number Correct	0	1	2	3	4

Skill	Circle the correct words.	Is it correct?				
D. Talk about holidays and special days in the U.S.	13. People vote on **Presidents' Day** / **Election Day**. 14. People usually watch **fireworks** / **television** on Independence Day. 15. Mothers' Day is in **March** / **May**. 16. My son will finish high school next week. I'm going to have a **graduation** / **Independence Day** party for him.	☐ ☐ ☐ ☐				
	Number Correct	0	1	2	3	4

COUNT the number of correct answers above. Fill in the circles.

Chart Your Success					
Skill	Needs Practice	Needs Practice	Okay	Very Good	Excellent!
A. Make sentences and ask questions about the future with *be going to*.	⓪	①	②	③	④
B. Make sentences with *might* **and** *might not*.	⓪	①	②	③	④
C. Talk about plans for the weekend.	⓪	①	②	③	④
D. Talk about holidays and special days in the U.S.	⓪	①	②	③	④

LESSON 1: Grammar and Vocabulary

 1 **GRAMMAR PICTURE DICTIONARY.** Listen and repeat.

TCD4, 31
SCD, 65

1
I want to **become** a **citizen**. That is my **goal**.

2
Citizenship Requirements
- Live in U.S. for 5 years
- Be 18 years old
- Pay taxes
- Be a legal resident

First, I need to learn the **citizenship requirements**.

3
Application for Naturalization Form N-400

Next, I need to fill out the **naturalization application**.

4
Immigration and Naturalization Service

I need to take a **citizenship test** and **pass the citizenship interview**.

5
I also need to **pass a background check**.

6
I plan to take the **Oath of Allegiance** sometime next year.

7
Then I plan to **vote in elections**.

8
I also want to travel with a U.S. **passport**.

9
I plan to **volunteer** in my community and be a good citizen.

2 **NOTICE THE GRAMMAR.** Look at Activity 1. Underline _to_ and the verb after _to_.

Using Infinitives

We use infinitives to talk about goals, plans, and needs.

Affirmative Statements

Subject	Verb	Infinitive
I You	want plan need	to vote. to travel.
We You They		
He She	wants plans needs	

Negative Statements

Subject	Verb		Infinitive
I You	don't	want plan need	to vote. to travel.
We You They			
He She	doesn't		

3 **WRITE.** Put the words in the correct order.

1. pass / the / test / citizenship / need / You / to / .

   You need to pass the citizenship test.

2. We / passports / plan / don't / get / to / .

   _____

3. volunteer / to / They / want / the / in / community / .

   _____

4. pass / needs / background check / He / to / a / .

   _____

5. Oath of Allegiance / doesn't / take / to / want / She / the / .

   _____

6. to / the / She / fill / application / plan / out / doesn't / .

   _____

4 **WHAT ABOUT YOU?** Circle words to make sentences that are true about you.

1. I **plan to / don't plan to** get a passport.

2. I **need to / don't need to** learn more English.

3. I **want to / don't want to** fill out the citizenship application.

4. I **plan to / don't plan to** vote in elections.

5. I **want to / don't want to** volunteer in my community.

TALK. Read your sentences to a partner.

LESSON 2: Grammar Practice Plus

1 **LOOK** at the picture. The students are thinking about their future goals. What does each person want to do? Write the numbers from the picture next to the goals.

> Maria wants to get a job.

Goals

_2_ get a job

____ graduate from college

____ purchase a home

____ send children to college

____ be a pharmacist

  LISTEN. Are your answers correct?

TCD4, 32

2 **WHAT ABOUT YOU?** Talk with a partner. Ask and answer questions about the picture.

> What does Maria want to do?
>
> She wants to get a job.
>
> What do Joseph and Sara plan to do?
>
> They plan to buy a house.

3 **WHAT ABOUT YOU?** Check ☑ the things you want to do. Then ask your partner the questions and check ☑ your partner's answers.

Do you want . . .	Me	My Partner
1. to become a citizen?	☐	☐
2. to purchase a home?	☐	☐
3. to learn more English?	☐	☐
4. to get a job?	☐	☐
5. to get married?	☐	☐
6. to be a teacher?	☐	☐
7. to go to college?	☐	☐
8. to send your children to college?	☐	☐

WRITE. Complete the sentences using the information in Activity 3.

1. My partner wants to _____.

2. I don't want to _____.

3. My partner _____ be a teacher.

4. I _____ learn more English.

5. My partner and I _____.

6. My partner _____.

4 **TALK.** Ask your classmates about their goals. Take notes.

Name	Goal
Henry	*be a teacher*

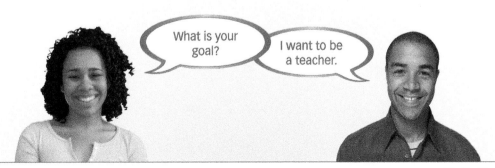

What is your goal?

I want to be a teacher.

LESSON 3: Listening and Conversation

1 **LISTEN.** Write the number of each speaker next to the pictures.

TCD4, 33
SCD, 66

TCD4, 34

2 **LISTEN** to the question. Then listen to the conversation.
Fill in the circle for the correct answer.

1. (A)   (B)   (C)   3. (A)   (B)   (C)

2. (A)   (B)   (C)   4. (A)   (B)   (C)

TCD4, 35

3 **LISTEN** to the first part of a conversation. Then listen to three possible answers
to finish the conversation. Fill in the circle for the correct answer.

1. (A)   (B)   (C)   4. (A)   (B)   (C)

2. (A)   (B)   (C)   5. (A)   (B)   (C)

3. (A)   (B)   (C)   6. (A)   (B)   (C)

Share personal and professional goals.

4 **LISTEN** and read.

TCD4, 36
SCD, 67

A: What is your goal?

B: I want to be a pharmacist.

A: What is your first step?

B: First, I need to finish my English classes.

A: What do you plan to do after that?

B: Next, I plan to go to college.

A: That sounds like a good plan. Good luck!

LISTEN AGAIN and repeat. Then practice with a partner.

TCD4, 37

* First step = first thing to do in a plan

5 **PRACTICE THE CONVERSATION** with a partner.

Goal	1. get a driver's license	2. become a citizen	3. go to college
First Step	learn to drive	take a citizenship class	complete my GED
Next Step	take a driving test	fill out the naturalization application	apply to a colleges

6 **WHAT ABOUT YOU?** Walk around the room and talk to your classmates. Ask about goals. Write names next to goals in the chart. Then ask about first steps. Complete the chart. Write notes.

Pete, do you want to get a high school diploma?

What is your first step?

Yes, I do.

First, I need to finish my English classes.

Do you want to . . . ?	Name	What is your first step?
get a high school diploma	Pete	Finish my English classes
1. become a citizen		
2. go to college		
3. get a GED		
4. get a driver's license		
5. find a job		
6. get married		
7. move up at work		

LESSON 4: Grammar and Vocabulary

 1 **GRAMMAR PICTURE DICTIONARY.** Listen and repeat.

TCD4, 38
SCD, 68

1
Next January, I will complete my English course.

2
I will **earn** a **certificate of completion**.

3
After that, I will get a job and **save money** for college **tuition**.

4
I will also apply for a **student loan** next spring.

5
I will try to **get good grades**.

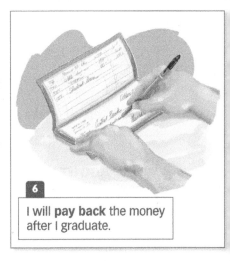

6
I will **pay back** the money after I graduate.

7
It won't be easy to **reach** my goal, but I will work hard.

8
I'll be very happy at my **graduation**.

9
Someday, I'll be **proud** of my **success**.

2 **NOTICE THE GRAMMAR.** Look at Activity 1. Circle the verbs. Underline the time expressions.

Future with *will*

Use *will* to talk about promises and what you think will happen in the future.

Affirmative Statements

Subject	*will*	base verb	
I You He She We They	will	pay back	the money.
College	will	be	difficult.

Negative Statements

Subject	*won't*	base verb	
I You He She We They	won't	be	late.
College	won't	be	easy.

3 **WRITE** the sentences. Use the correct form of *will*.

1. Next month, I _____ *will become* _____ (become) a U.S. citizen.

2. The class _____ (not start) next week.

3. Paula _____ (not be) ready to leave at 8:00.

4. Hakan and Julia _____ (get married) next year.

5. Someday, we _____ (buy) a house.

6. He _____ (not be) late for class.

4 **WHAT ABOUT YOU?** Choose three of the activities below. Write sentences about your future. Use *will* or *won't*.

~~get married~~	buy a house	graduate from college	get a good job

1. *I will get married in five years.* _____

2. _____

3. _____

4. _____

TALK. Read your sentences to a partner.

LESSON 5: Grammar Practice Plus

 A **LISTEN.** Circle the words you hear.

TCD4, 39
SCD, 69

1. **She'll** / **I'll** travel to China next week.
2. **He'll / She'll** start a business next year.
3. **We'll / I'll** graduate in June.
4. **You'll / I'll** be a good citizen.

5. **You'll / They'll** get married in six months.
6. **She'll / We'll** vote in every election.
7. **It'll / I'll** start at 8:30.
8. **I'll / You'll** be happy.

 B **LISTEN AGAIN** and repeat.

TCD4, 40
SCD, 70

 C **LISTEN.** Which do you hear? Circle *will* or *won't*.

TCD4, 41
SCD, 71

1. will	won't		5. will	won't
2. will	won't		6. will	won't
3. will	won't		7. will	won't
4. will	won't		8. will	won't

1 **MATCH** the words with the definitions.

1. _____ application deadline
2. _____ application process
3. _____ financial aid
4. _____ student loan
5. _____ scholarship
6. _____ semester

a. part of a school year. In some schools, semesters are nine weeks. In other schools, semesters are 12 weeks.

b. money for college that comes from a school or from the government. Financial aid can be a loan or a scholarship.

c. things you have to do, like filling out papers, to apply for something

d. the last date you can apply for something

e. Money for tuition and other expenses. Students do not pay back the money. Colleges and organizations often give scholarships to excellent students, and to students who need help to pay for college.

f. money that students borrow for college. After graduation, students pay back the money.

2 **READ** the information about financial aid for college. Underline these words:

application process	deadline	~~financial aid~~	scholarships	semester	student loans

Learn About Financial Aid!

Are you interested in <u>financial aid</u> for fall semester?

Come to the Financial Aid Workshop.
April 22   3:00–5:00 P.M.
Morgan Library, Room 317

Learn about:
- **Scholarships** *Who can apply?*
- **Student loans** *How much money can you borrow?*
- **Application process** *What are the requirements?*
- **Application deadline** *When is it due?*

3 **WRITE.** Complete the sentences. Use words from Activity 2.

1. *A:* My sister and I want to go to college next year, but we don't have money for tuition.

   B: Will you apply for _____ from the government?

2. *A:* When does the fall _____ start?

   B: It starts September 5th.

3. *A:* Mary is going to go to college next year. She got a _____ from the school.

   B: That's wonderful! She won't have to pay back the money after she graduates.

4. *A:* When is the application _____?

   B: It's due May 31st. After May 31st, you cannot apply for financial aid for the fall semester.

5. *A:* What is the _____?

   B: First, fill out the papers. Then mail your application to the financial aid office.

4 **WHAT ABOUT YOU?** Write the answers to the questions.

1. How will you practice English after your class is done? _____

2. Which of your classmates will go to college in the future? _____

3. What kind of job will you have in five years? _____

4. Where will you live in ten years? _____

TALK. Ask and answer the questions with a partner.

LESSON 6: Apply Your Knowledge

1 **READ** Michael's application to West City College. What is his educational goal?

West City College Application for Enrollment

Name: *Michael Moran*

Address: *318 Pine Street, Dallas, TX 75225*

---

1. What is your ethnic background?

   ☐ Asian   ☒ Hispanic   ☐ White non-Hispanic   ☐ Other non-white   ☐ Other _____

2. What is your citizenship status?

   ☐ Temporary resident   ☒ U.S. citizen   ☐ Refugee   ☐ Student visa   ☐ Other

3. Are you the first person in your family to attend college? ☐ yes   ☒ no

4. Did you graduate from high school or do you have a GED certificate? ☒ yes   ☐ no

5. Did you attend this college or another college before? ☐ yes   ☒ no

6. What is your educational goal?

   ☐ Two-year college degree   ☒ Four-year college degree   ☐ Not sure

7. Are you going to work during the next semester of college? ☒ yes   ☐ no

   If yes, how many hours per week? __*20*__

8. Will you need financial aid? ☒ yes   ☐ no

WRITE short answers to the questions.

1. Is Michael the first person in his family to go to college? *No, he isn't.* _____

2. Did he finish high school? _____

3. Does he want to earn a four-year college degree? _____

4. Is he going to work next semester? _____

Math: Calculate to Save Money

Marcus needs to save $5,000 in the next three years because he wants to send his son to community college. How much money does he need to save each month?

Multiply: 3 years X 12 months = _____ months

Divide: $5,000 ÷ (number of months) = $ _____ per month

Answer: Marcus needs to save _____ dollars each month for the next three years.

Complete an enrollment application. • Calculate saving money. • Meet with a college counselor.

2 **LISTEN** and read.

TCD4, 42
SCD, 72

Counselor:	What is your educational goal?
Student:	I plan to get a four-year college degree.
Counselor:	And what is your career goal?
Student:	I want to be a restaurant manager.
Counselor:	Did you finish high school?
Student:	Yes, I did. I earned a GED certificate.
Counselor:	You need to take an English test. Please call the admissions office and make an appointment.
Student:	Thanks. I'll call right away.

LISTEN AGAIN and repeat. Then practice with a partner.

TCD4, 43

3 **PRACTICE THE CONVERSATION** from Activity 2 with a partner.

1 four-year college degree/
pharmacist/
have a high school diploma

2 two-year college degree/
child-care worker/
completed six years of secondary school

3 job-training certificate/
auto mechanic/
earned a GED certificate

4 four-year college degree/
librarian/
have a high school diploma

4 **WHAT ABOUT YOU?** Write information about your goals and education in the chart. Then talk with a partner and take notes.

	Educational goal	Career goal	Educational history
You			
Your partner			

LESSON 7: Reading

1 THINK ABOUT IT. Do you have a personal goal? When will you reach your goal? Will it be easy or difficult?

2 BEFORE YOU READ. Look at the picture and title of the article. What is the reading about?

3 READ the article. <u>Underline</u> Luisa's goal.

Local Immigrant Will Reach Life Goal

Baker, CA – When Luisa Gonzales was a young girl, she dreamed about going to college. She grew up in a small village in Colombia, and her family was very poor. When Luisa was 19 years old, Luisa's family moved to the United States. In the beginning, their life was very difficult. Luisa worked every day as a seamstress and gave her salary to her family. She didn't learn much English. When Luisa was 30, she decided to begin the steps to reach her goal. She wanted to get a college degree. First, she needed to learn English. She studied English at night at Baker Adult School. A year later, she started classes at Baker State College. Now, she is studying hard in college and she is a very good student. She goes to school every day and never misses class. Next week, she is going to graduate from college. After that, she is going to look for a job. Luisa is very excited about her graduation. She is very proud of her success.

Luisa Gonzales will graduate from Baker State College next week.

4 WRITE the details from the reading in the chart below. Use these words.

learned English in adult school	going to graduate from college	~~moved to the United States~~	goes to class every day
going to look for a job	enrolled at Baker State College	is studying hard in college	

Steps completed in the past	Current steps	Future steps
moved to the U.S.		

Writing

1 **PLAN AHEAD.** Answer the questions.

a. What is your goal? _____

b. When do you plan to complete the goal? (Write a year or month) _____

Writing Tip

Always **plan** your writing before you begin to write. Charts can help you organize your ideas.

2 **BEFORE YOU WRITE.** Plan your paragraph. In the chart, write the steps to reach your goal.

Completed steps	Current steps	Future steps

3 **WRITE** a paragraph about your goal and your steps to reach it. Write about one step you finished in the past, one step you are doing now, and one step you plan to do in the future. Finally, write a title for the paragraph.

_____

_____

_____

_____

_____

_____

_____

_____

_____

_____

4 **EDIT** your paragraph. Circle *Yes* or *No*.

1. Did you indent the first sentence?   Yes   No

2. Do you have a title?   Yes   No

3. Does each sentence begin with a capital
   letter and end with a period?   Yes   No

4. Is your writing neat and easy to read?   Yes   No

1 READ AND LISTEN. Then practice with a partner.

TCD4, 44

1

Let's make sure we remembered everything.

OK. Maggie is going to bring balloons. Sofia has the gift for Lena. Chef Alfonso is baking the cake.

2

Mmm. I can smell that cake.

Excellent! We can put up all of the decorations before Lena arrives!

3

Thank you all so much. You're wonderful people to work with. I'll miss you very much. But this party is not only for me!

4

Congratulations, Oscar! You worked hard and made a lot of good changes here. You're going to be the new manager.

Congratulations, Oscar!

Wow. Thanks everyone!

2 TALK with a partner. Answer the questions.

1. What are Oscar and Eric doing?
2. What is Sofia's responsibility?
3. What is Maggie going to bring?
4. What is Chef Alfonso doing?
5. Why is Lena going to miss everyone?
6. What is Lena's news?

3 WHAT ABOUT YOU? Do you have parties for coworkers or friends? What kinds of parties do you have (anniversary, graduation, new positiion at work, new baby)? What do you do to prepare for the party? Do you like to have parties at home, at a restaurant, or in a park?

Check Your Progress!

Skill	Circle the correct words.	Is it correct?
A. Use infinitives to talk about future plans.	1. He wants **to become**/**to becomes** a citizen. 2. She **needs to pass**/**needs pass** the citizenship test. 3. I plan **to take**/**take** the Oath of Allegiance sometimes next year. 4. I **going to**/**am going to** invite my friend to dinner.	○ ○ ○ ○

		Number Correct	0	1	2	3	4

Skill	Circle the correct words.	Is it correct?
B. Use *will* and *won't* to talk about future plans.	5. What will she do next year? **She'll**/**He'll** look for a job. 6. It's going to be cold this weekend. I **won't**/**not will** go to the beach. 7. After they graduate next year, Joan and Bill **will go**/**go** to college. 8. A: Where will you live in ten years. B: I **will living**/**will live** in Los Angeles.	○ ○ ○ ○

		Number Correct	0	1	2	3	4

Skill	Circle the correct words.	Is it correct?
C. Talk about goals.	9. I want to travel to many countries. I need a **U.S. Certificate**/**U.S. passport**. 10. I want to be a pharmacist. That is my **career**/**educational** goal. 11. I want to graduate. That is my **career**/**educational** goal. 12. I didn't finish high school. Now, I want to earn a **GED**/**semester**.	○ ○ ○ ○

		Number Correct	0	1	2	3	4

Skill	Circle the correct words.	Is it correct?
D. Apply for financial aid for college.	13. I need money for college. I will apply for **health aid**/**financial aid**. 14. The deadline is the **first**/**last** day you can apply for a student loan. 15. I **have to**/**don't have to** pay back my student loan. 16. I **have to**/**don't have to** pay back my scholarship.	○ ○ ○ ○

		Number Correct	0	1	2	3	4

COUNT the number of correct answers above. Fill in the circles.

Chart Your Success

Skill	Needs Practice	Needs Practice	Okay	Very Good	Excellent!
A. Use *will* and *won't* to talk about future plans.	⓪	①	②	③	④
B. Use *will* and *won't* to talk about future plans.	⓪	①	②	③	④
C. Talk about goals.	⓪	①	②	③	④
D. Apply for financial aid for college.	⓪	①	②	③	④

Information Gap Activity

Unit 4 LESSON 4 Activity 6, page 65

Student B: Use the information below to answer Student A's questions.

Job Responsibilities: The sales manager trains new sales peoples and makes the work schedule each week.

Experience: The person who takes the job needs to have two years of experience or more as a manager.

Salary: The salary for the Sales Manager position is between $35,000 and $45,000 depending on your experience.

Work schedule: The position will be available starting on October 12th.

Benefits: The company offers health insurance, and two weeks of vacation.

How/apply: To apply for the job, come into the company and fill out an application.

Unit 6 LESSON 6 Activity 5, page 97

Student B: Ask and answer questions about Martin's work schedule and complete the chart.

Employee: *Martin Salcedo*		Date: *February 20*		
Monday	**Tuesday**	**Wednesday**	**Thursday**	**Friday**
	3:00–10:00 *(Dinner 7:00–8:00)*			*2:00–8:00* *(Dinner 4:00–5:00)*

Unit 7 LESSON 6 Activity B, page 112

Student A: 1. The population of Mitchell is 73,922.

2. The average salary in Mitchell is $43,656.

3. The average price of a 3-bedroom house in Mitchell is $99,652.

Student B: 1. The population of Reston is 32,656.

2. The average salary in Reston is $39,720.

3. The average price of a 3-bedroom house in Reston is $88,541.

Unit 9 LESSON 6 Activity 6, page 145

Student B: Use the information below to answer Student A's questions.

> Cupcake Bakery is the best bakery in town. It is located at 22 Pine Street.
>
> The bakery is open from 6:00 a.m. to 6:00 p.m..The prices are very reasonable:
>
> cakes $9.50; bread $3.75 per loaf; cookies $9.00 per pound.

Grammar Reference Guide

Nouns

Quantifiers

We use quantifiers to talk about the number or amount of something.

Quantifier	Count Noun
a	carrot
an	apple
two	oranges
a couple of	lemons
a few	peppers
some	eggs
several	onions
a lot of	bananas

Quantifier	Non-Count Noun
	protein
	spinach
	salt
a little bit of	coffee
some	
	tuna
a lot of	chicken
	cereal
	milk

Questions and Statements with Count Nouns and Non-Count Nouns

Affirmative Statements

count	There are	**many**	calories in the cookies.
non-count	There is	**some**	calcium in the cookies.

Negative Statements

count	There aren't	**any**	vitamins in the cookies.
non-count	There isn't	**any**	iron in the cookies.

Questions

count	Are there Are there	**any** **many**	vitamins in the cookies? calories?
non-count	Is there Is there	**any** **much**	iron in the cookies? calcium?

Adjectives

Comparative Adjectives

We use comparative adjectives to compare two nouns.

Adjective	Comparative Adjective
My old neighborhood was **noisy**.	My new neighborhood is **noisier**.

Using *than*

Subject + Verb	Comparative Adjective	*than*	Noun
My hometown was Houses in my new town are	bigger more expensive	than	my new town. houses in my hometown.

Rules	Examples
1. Add *-er* or *-r* to most **one-syllable adjectives**.	old**er** larg**er**
2. For most **one-syllable adjectives ending in consonant + vowel + consonant**, double the consonant and add *-er*. Do not double *w*.	big**ger** new**er**
3. For **two-syllable adjectives ending in y**, change the *y* to *i* and add *-er*.	sunny ⟶ sunn**ier** noisy ⟶ nois**ier**
4. For **adjectives with two or more syllables that do *not* end in y**, use the word *more*.	**more** relaxed **more** stressful
5. Some comparative adjectives are **irregular**. See page xx for a list of irregular adjectives.	good ⟶ **better** bad ⟶ **worse**

Superlative Adjectives

We use superlative adjectives to compare three or more people, places, or things.

Adjective	Comparative Adjective	Superlative Adjective
Eve's house is **large**.	Tim's house is **larger than** Eve's house.	Alan's house is **the largest** of the three houses.

Rules	Examples
Add *-est* or *-st* to most **one-syllable adjectives**.	the old**est** the safe**st**
For **one-syllable adjectives ending in consonant + vowel + consonant**, double the consonant and add *-est*.	the big**gest** the thin**nest**
For **two-syllable adjectives ending in -y**, change the *-y* to *i* and add *-est*.	busy ⟶ bus**iest** noisy ⟶ nois**iest**
For adjectives with **two or more syllables that do *not* end in -y**, use the words *the most*.	**the most** expensive **the most** dangerous
Some adjectives have **irregular** superlative forms.	good ⟶ **the best** bad ⟶ **the worst**

Adverbs

Adverbs of Frequency

Adverbs of frequency usually come after the subject and before the verb.

Subject	Adverb of Frequency	Verb	
I You He She We You They	always (100%) usually sometimes rarely never (0%)	speak(s)	in English. in Spanish. in Chinese. in French.

Expressions of Frequency

Expressions of frequency usually come at the end of a sentence.

Subject	Verb	Expression of Frequency
I You	study	every day. every weekend.
He She	takes a test	every month. every year.
We You They	check email	once a day. twice a day. three times a day.

Verbs

Present Continuous Statements

We use the present continuous to talk about actions happening right now.

Affirmative				Negative		
Subject	be	Verb + ing		Subject	be + not	Verb + ing
I	am	standing. walking. working.		I	'm not	sitting. running. sleeping.
You	are			You	aren't	
He She	is			He She	isn't	
We You They	are			We You They	aren't	

Spelling rules:

1. Add -ing to most verbs: **study – studying   mail – mailing   play – playing**
2. Words with *consonant + -e*, drop -e and add -ing: **take – taking   use – using**
3. Words with *vowel + one consonant*, double the consonant and add –ing:
   run – running   stop – stopping

Present Continuous Questions

Yes/No Questions

Be	Subject	Verb + *ing*
Am	I	
Are	you	
Is	he / she	learning? waiting? working?
Are	we / you / they	

Answers

	Subject	Verb
	I	am.
	you	are.
Yes,	he / she	is.
	we / you / they	are.

	Subject	Verb + *not*
	I	'm not.
	you	aren't.
No,	he / she	isn't.
	we / you / they	aren't.

Information Questions

Question Word	*be*	Subject	Verb + *ing*
What	are	you	doing?
Where	is	he	going?
Why	is	the bank	closing?

Answers

I'm making a deposit.
To the library.
Because it is 5:00.

Polite Requests and Offers

We use the modals *can*, *could*, *may*, and *would* to make polite requests and offers. *Could*, *may*, and *might* are more polite than *can*.

Requests

Modal	Subject	Verb	
Can **Could** **Would**	you	help	me?
Can **Could** **May**	I	have	a box?

Answers

Affirmative	Negative
Sure.	I'm sorry, I'm busy.
Of course. Yes, you can.	I'm sorry, we don't have boxes.

Offers

Modal	Subject	Verb	
Can **Could** **May**	I	help	you?

Answers

Affirmative	Negative
Yes, please.	No, thank you.

Simple Present Tense

We use simple present to talk about activities that we do again and again.

Affirmative

Subject	Verb	
I You	relax	
He She	relaxes	in the morning. on Monday.
We You They	relax	

Negative

Subject	do + not	Verb	
I You	don't		
He She	doesn't	relax	in the morning. on Monday.
We You They	don't		

Spelling rules for simple present:

1. Add -s to the base form of a verb (for *He, She, It*): start → start**s**,   walk → walk**s**
2. For verbs ending in consonant + -y, change -y to -i and add -es: study → stud**ies**, carry → carr**ies**
3. For verbs ending in vowel + -y, add -s: buy → buy**s**,   pay → pay**s**
4. For verbs ending in -s, -z, -ch, -sh, and -x, add -es: relax → relax**es**, watch → watch**es**

Simple Present Tense: *Yes/No* Questions and Answers

Questions

Do	Subject	Verb
Do	I you	
Does	he she it	work?
Do	we you they	

Answers

	Subject	do
Yes,	I you	do.
	he she it	does.
	we you they	do.

	Subject	do
No,	I you	don't.
	he she it	doesn't.
	we you they	don't.

Simple Present Tense: Information Questions

To ask for information, use: *who, what, where, when, why,* and *how*.

Information Questions

Question Word	do/does	Subject	Verb
Where	do	you	work?
When			
What	does	it	cost?
Who	does	he/she	work with?
Why	do	they	go home early?
How	do	they	get to work?
How much	do	they	pay for overtime?

Answers

I work at Spencer Hospital.
I work the night shift.
It costs $20.
He/She works with Fred.
Because they start work early.
They take the bus.
They pay $14.50 per hour.

Simple Past Tense of Regular Verbs

We use the simple past tense to talk about actions completed in the past.

Affirmative			Negative			
Subject	Verb		Subject	*didn't*	Verb	
I You He She We You They	talked	to the doctor.	I You He She We You They	didn't	talk	to the nurse.

Spelling Rules

1. Add *-ed* or *-d* to most verbs. burn → burn**ed**, use → use**d**
2. If a verb ends in consonant + *y*, change the *y* to *i* and add *-ed*. stud**y** → stud**ied**
3. If a verb ends in vowel + *w*, *x*, or *y*, add *–ed*. sho**w** → show**ed**, fix → fix**ed**, stay → stay**ed**
4. If a one-syllable verb ends in consonant + vowel + consonant, double the consonant and add *-ed*. s**top** → stop**ped**, s**hop** → shop**ped**

Past Time Expressions

Time expressions tell when something happened.

	Past Time Expression
I had a doctor's appointment	on Tuesday. yesterday. three days ago.

Past Time Expressions		
this morning	at 8:00	last fall
yesterday	on Sunday	last winter
the day before yesterday	in June	last weekend
two days ago	in 2005	last month
three years ago	last summer	last year
		last night

Simple Past Tense: *Yes/No* Questions and Answers

We use simple past questions to ask about actions in the past.

Question

Did	Subject	Verb	
	I		
	you		
	he		
Did	she	load	the boxes?
	we		
	you		
	they		

Affirmative

	Subject	did	
	I		
	you		
	he		
Yes,	she	did.	
	we		
	you		
	they		

Negative

	Subject	did + not	
	I		
	you		
	he		
No,	she	didn't.	
	we		
	you		
	they		

Simple Past Tense: Information Questions

Use question words to ask for information about the past.

Questions

Question Word	did	Subject	Verb	
How	did	I	do?	
When	did	you	leave	your last job?
Where	did	he/she	learn	to drive?
What	did	we	forget	to do at work?
Who	did	you	ask	to the party?
Why	did	they	leave	their jobs?

Answers

Subject	Verb	
You	did	very well.
I	left	my last job in March.
He/She	learned	to drive in Mexico.
You	forgot	to repair the window.
We	asked	the manager.
They	left	because of the pay.

Simple Past of *Be*: Statements and Questions

Use the simple past tense of *be* to talk about things that started and ended in the past.

Affirmative Statements

Subject	was/were	
I	was	uncomfortable. excited. calm. nervous.
You	were	
She	was	
We	were	

Negative Statements

Subject	was/were not	
I	wasn't	uncomfortable. excited. calm. nervous.
You	weren't	
She	wasn't	
We	weren't	

Yes/No Questions

Was/Were	Subject	
Was	I	late? angry? in L.A. last month?
Was	he	
Were	you	

Information Questions

Question Word	was/were	Subject	
What	was	his	job?
Why	were	you	late?
When	were	you	in Spain?
Where	was	he	today?
Who	was	she	with?
How	was	your	trip?

Information Questions with *Be* and *Do*

Question Word	*be*	Adjective + Subject
Where	is	the closest bus stop?
Who	is	your plumber?
How much	are	these chairs?

Question Word	*do*	Subject	Verb
Where	does	this bus	go?
Who	does	he	need?
How much	do	these chairs	cost?

Which + Noun	*be*	Adjective
Which store	is	the best?

Which + Noun	*do*	Subject	Verb
Which store	do	you	like?

Have to and *Must*

We use *have to* + verb and *must* + verb to say that something is necessary.

Affirmative

We usually use *have to* when we speak.

Subject	have to/has to	
I You We They	have to	take the driving test.
He She	has to	

Negative

Don't have to means something isn't necessary.

Subject	*don't have to/ doesn't have to*	
I You We They	don't have to	take the driving test.
He She	doesn't have to	

Affirmative

We usually use *must* to talk about rules and laws.

Subject	*must*	
I You He She We You They	must	wear a seatbelt.

Negative

Must not means it's important NOT to do something.

Subject	*must not (musn't)*	
I You He She We You They	must not (mustn't)	drive too fast.

Imperatives

We use imperative sentences to tell people to do things (commands) and to give directions.

Affirmative Imperatives

Turn right at the traffic light and **go** toward the park.
Go through the park, and **walk** north for two blocks.

Negative Imperatives

Don't go into the parking lot.
Don't turn left.

The Future with *Be Going to*

Use *be going to* to talk about future plans.

Affirmative and Negative Statements

Subject + *be*	*(not) going to*	Verb
I'm		
She's		
You're	going to **not going to**	study. go hiking.
We're		
They're		

The Future with *Might*

Use *might* to talk about future possibilities (when you are not sure).

Affirmative Statements

Subject	*might*	Verb
I You He She We You They	**might**	go out.

Negative Statements

Subject	*might not*	Verb
I You He She We You They	**might not**	go out.

Using Infinitives

We use infinitives to talk about goals, plans, and needs.

Affirmative Statements

Subject	Verb	Infinitive
I You We You They	want plan need	**to vote.** **to travel.**
He She	wants plans needs	

Negative Statements

Subject	Verb		Infinitive
I You We You They	don't	want plan need	**to vote.** **to travel.**
He She	doesn't		

Future with *will*

Use *will* to talk about promises and what you think will happen in the future.

Affirmative Statements

Subject	will	base verb	
I You He She We They	will	pay back	the money.
College	will	be	difficult.

Negative Statements

Subject	won't	base verb	
I You He She We They	won't	be	late.
College	won't	be	easy.

Irregular Past Tense Verbs

Present		Simple Past	
be	lend	was/were	lent
become	lose	became	lost
begin	make	began	made
break	meet	broke	met
bring	pay	brought	paid
buy	put	bought	put
catch	read	caught	read
choose	ride	chose	rode
come	run	came	ran
cost	say	cost	said
do	see	did	saw
draw	sell	drew	sold
drink	send	drank	sent
drive	shut	drove	shut
eat	sing	ate	sang
fall	sleep	fell	slept
feel	speak	felt	spoke
fight	spend	fought	spent
find	stand	found	stood
fly	steal	flew	stole
forget	swim	forgot	swam
get	take	got	took
give	teach	give	taught
go	tell	went	told
grow	think	grew	thought
have	throw	had	thought
hear	throw	heard	threw
hit	understand	hit	understood
keep	wake	kept	woke
know	wear	knew	wore
leave	win	left	won
	write		wrote

Audio Script

NOTE: This audio script offers support for many of the activities in the Student Book. When the words on the Student Book page are identical to those on the audio program, the script is not provided here.

Pre-Unit
Activity 7 (page 3)
1. *A:* What does excellent mean?
   B: Excellent means very, very good.
2. *A:* Is my answer correct?
   B: Yes, your answer is correct!
3. *A:* How do you spell Florida?
   B: F-L-O-R-I-D- A
4. *A:* Can you repeat that?
   B: I said, "The address is 293 Elm Street".
5. *A:* May I work with you?
   B: Sure. I'd like to work with you.
6. *A:* Could I borrow your pencil?
   B: Yes, of course. You can borrow my pencil.

UNIT 1
LESSON 2 Activity 5 (page 9)
1. It's Clara's birthday today. She is seven years old. She has long, curly brown hair.
2. Jose is Clara's younger brother. He is only two years old. He has short brown hair and brown eyes. He also has freckles.
3. Laura is tall and thin. She has straight brown hair and glasses.
4. Sofia has blonde hair and blue eyes. She is pregnant.
5. Pablo is short and has brown hair. He has a mustache.

LESSON 3 Activity 1 (page 10)
1. Attention shoppers! We have a lost child in the customer service department. She has straight black hair and brown eyes. Her name is Lian.

   Where are these people?
   A. at a school
   B. at a store
   C. at a park

2. Attention shoppers! There is a lost child in the store. She is four years old and has long brown hair and brown eyes. Her name is Karima. If you see her, please bring her to the customer service department.

   What is the announcement about?
   A. a sale in the children's department
   B. a phone call for the shoe department
   C. a lost child

3. Attention shoppers! We have a lost child in the customer service department. She is tall and thin. She has short blonde hair and green eyes. Her name is Mary. Will Mary's parents please come to customer service?

   What color is Mary's hair?
   A. blonde
   B. brown
   C. black

4. Attention shoppers! There is a lost child in the store. Her name is Julia. She is eight years old and has curly black hair and brown eyes. She also has freckles. If you see her, please bring her to the customer service department.

   How old is the child?
   A. six years old
   B. eight years old
   C. 18 years old

LESSON 5 Pronunciation Activity A (page 15)
1. My daughter's birthday is March thirtieth.
2. My son is thirteen years old.
3. There are thirty students in the class.
4. She is in the third grade.
5. The principal's office is in room seventy.
6. The high school is on Eightieth Street.

UNIT 2
LESSON 2 Activity 4 (page 25)
1. *A:* What are Li Ping and Chen doing?
   B: They're talking and walking.
2. *A:* What are Sara and Todd doing?
   B: They're waiting in line for the ATM.
3. *A:* What is Sharon doing?
   B: She's applying for a checking account.
4. *A:* What is Tim doing?
   B: He's buying new shoes.
5. *A:* What is Bob doing?
   B: He's withdrawing cash from the ATM.
6. *A:* What is Joe doing?
   B: He's mailing a letter.

LESSON 3 Activity 2 (page 26)
1. *A:* Good afternoon, Jamestown Medical Center.
   B: Hi. Could I speak to Dr. Richards?
   A: I'm sorry, Dr. Richards is having lunch in the cafeteria right now.
   B: Okay, I'll call back later.
   A: Okay, good-bye.
2. *A:* Hello? Memorial Middle School.
   B: Is Ms. Bell there?
   A: I'm sorry, she's busy right now. She's teaching English class.
   B: Okay, thank you.
3. *A:* Hello?
   B: Hi, Rick. It's Henry. Is Jennifer there?
   A: Hi, Henry. Sorry, Jennifer isn't here. She's buying a new coat.
   B: Okay, I'll call back tonight.
4. *A:* Dr. Bloom's office.
   B: May I speak to Dr. Bloom?
   A: I'm sorry, he's talking to a patient. Could you call again at 2:00 [two] p.m.?
   B: Sure. Thank you.
5. *A:* Antonio's Barber Shop.
   B: Hi. May I speak with Antonio?
   A: I'm sorry, he's not here. He's mailing a package at the post office. Call back in a few minutes.
   B: Okay. Thank you.

Activity 3 (page 26)
1. *A:* Hello. Mary speaking.
   B: Hi, Mary. This is Grandma Lee. May I speak to your mother?
   A: Mother isn't home. She's at the bank. She's cashing a check.
   B: Okay. Thanks. I'll call her again later.

   Why is the grandmother calling?
   A. She wants to talk to Mary's mother.
   B. She's at the bank.
   C. She isn't home.

2. *A:* Hello. Mary speaking.
   B: Hi, Mary. This is Grandma Lee. May I speak to your mother?
   A: Mother isn't home. She's at the bank. She's cashing a check.
   B: Okay. Thanks. I'll call her again later.

What is Mary's mother doing?
A. She's calling her friend.
B. She's cashing a check.
C. She isn't home.

3. *A:* Hello.
   B: Good morning, this is the Spencer Health Clinic. May I speak to Bob Smith?
   A: He isn't here. He's working.
   B: Okay, could you ask him to call the clinic, please?
   A: Sure.
   B: Thanks.

   Where is Bob Smith?
   A. He's at home.
   B. He's at work.
   C. He's at the health clinic.

4. *A:* Hello.
   B: Good morning, this is the Spencer Health Clinic. May I speak to Bob Smith?
   A: He isn't here. He's working.
   B: Okay, could you ask him to call the clinic, please?
   A: Sure.
   B: Thanks.

   Who is calling Bob Smith?
   A. Mr. Smith.
   B. His work.
   C. The health clinic.

5. *A:* Hello.
   B: Mrs. Smith? This is George. Could I speak to Matt?
   A: Matt isn't here. He's shopping. He's buying a present for his girlfriend. I think he's buying a diamond ring!
   B: Wow. That's exciting! Thanks, Mrs. Smith.

   What is Matt doing right now?
   A. He's talking to his girlfriend.
   B. He's shopping.
   C. He's talking on the phone.

6. *A:* Hello.
   B: Mrs. Smith? This is George. Could I speak to Matt?
   A: Matt isn't here. He's shopping. He's buying a present for his girlfriend. I think he's buying a diamond ring!
   B: Wow. That's exciting! Thanks, Mrs. Smith.

   What is Matt buying?
   A. A present for his girlfriend.
   B. A present for his mother.
   C. A ring for his father.

Pronunciation Activity B (page 31)
1. Could you help me?
2. Could I get a receipt?
3. Could he help me with my bags?
4. Could I smoke here?
5. Could she call me later?

LESSON 6 Activity 2 (page 32)
1. *A:* Can I check out a DVD?
   B: Yes, you can. You can check it out for two weeks.
2. *A:* Could I renew this book?
   B: Yes, of course. You can renew it once.
3. *A:* Could I check out this magazine?
   B: Yes, sure. You can check it out for a week.
4. *A:* Can I check out this book?
   B: No, I'm sorry. You can't.
5. *A:* May I renew this CD?
   B: Yes, of course. You can renew it once.

Unit 3

LESSON 2 Activity 1 (page 40)
1. On Wednesdays, Pete does laundry.
2. Andy and Becky send messages to friends and do homework.
3. Susan shops for food.
4. On Saturdays, Pete washes the car.
5. Susan goes to the gym.
6. Andy sleeps late.
7. Becky watches videos with her friend.

LESSON 3 Activity 1 (page 42)
1. *A:* I need an appointment with Mr. Brown.
   B: Can you come at three o'clock on Thursday?
   A: Yes, Thursday at three o'clock is fine.

   What time is the appointment?
   A. Thursday
   B. three o'clock
   C. an appointment

2. *A:* Lee's Beauty Shop.
   B: I need an appointment for a haircut.
   A: Can you come at 3:00 on Wednesday?

   What does the woman need?
   A. a haircut
   B. Wednesday
   C. three o'clock

3. *A:* Good morning. Central Elementary School.
   B: Hello. This is Mary Jones. I need to speak to my son's teacher.
   A: What is the teacher's name?
   B: My son's teacher is Mrs. Wilson.

   Who does the woman want to talk to?
   A. her daughter
   B. Mary Jones
   C. her son's teacher

4. *A:* Brown's Auto Shop
   B: I need an appointment for some car repairs.
   A: How about tomorrow at 8:30?
   B: That's fine.

   When is the appointment?
   A. in the afternoon
   B. nine thirty
   C. tomorrow

5. *A:* Wilson Plumbing.
   B: My toilet isn't working. I need someone to fix it.
   A: What's the problem?
   A: Water from the toilet is all over the floor!

   Who is the woman calling?
   A. the teacher
   B. nine thirty
   C. a plumber

6. *A:* I need an appointment with Mr. Lee.
   B: How about the fifteenth at two o'clock?
   A: That's good. Thank you.

   What is the date for the appointment?
   A. the fifteenth
   B. five o'clock
   C. the fifth

Activity 2 (page 42)
1. *A:* Good morning. Spencer Dental Office
   B: This is Jack Smith. I need an appointment for a check up.
   A: Are you free Tuesday at 4:30?
   B: Tuesday at 4:30? Sure. That's good. Thank you.

2. *A:* Hello. Linn's Beauty Shop.
   B: This is Sara McGee. I need an appointment for a hair cut.
   A: How about Monday at 8:30?
   B: Sorry. I go to school on Monday mornings.
   A: How about Monday at 12:30?
   B: Yes, that's fine. I can come at 12:30 on Monday. Thank you very much.

LESSON 6 Activity 1 (page 48)
A: Hi, My name is Leon. Welcome to our class.
B: Hi. I'm Samuel.
A: I'm the class helper today. I can help you fill out your registration form.
B: Thanks.
A: OK, so your first name is Samuel, right?
B: Samuel, that's right.
A: And your last name?
B: Mohammed.
A: Could you spell that, please?
B: Sure. It's M-O-H-A-M-M-E-D.
A: What's your address?
B: 4213 Elm Avenue, Los Angeles, California, 90034
A: And what's your nationality?
B: I'm Somali.
A: How many dependents do you have?
B: Dependents. Hmm. Well, there's my wife, and my four children. I have five dependents.

UNIT 4
LESSON 2 Activity 1 (page 56)
1. He's a cashier. He collects money and makes change.
2. He's a manager. He supervises workers.
3. He's a gardener. He takes care of plants.
4. He's a pilot. He flies airplanes.
5. She's a flight attendant. She helps passengers on flights.
6. They're airport security agents. They inspect luggage.

LESSON 3 Pronunciation Activity B (page 58)
1. Does he earn a good salary?
2. Does she collect money?
3. Does she supervise workers?
4. Does he assist with patients?
5. Does he inspect luggage?
6. Does she fly airplanes?

Activity 1 (page 58)
1. *A:* Do you work the day shift?
   B: No, I don't. I work the night shift from 3:00 [three] p.m. to midnight.

   What shift does the woman work?
   A. the night shift
   B. the day shift
   C. three o'clock

2. *A:* Do you work on weekends?
   B: Yes, I do. I work every Saturday from eight to five.

   Does the man work on weekends?
   A. No, he doesn't
   B. Yes, he does.
   C. No, it doesn't.

3. *A:* Tell me about your work experience.
   B: I have two years experience in restaurant work. I worked from 2006 to 2008 at Pat's Restaurant.

   Does the woman have work experience?
   A. No, she doesn't.
   B. 2008
   C. Yes, she does.

4. *A:* My pay is very low. I only earn six dollars per hour.
   B: That's too bad.

   Does the woman earn a good salary?
   A. Yes, she does.
   B. No, she doesn't.
   C. Six dollars per hour

5. *A:* Does the work schedule include weekends?
   B: No, it doesn't. The work schedule is Monday through Friday.

   What is the conversation about?
   A. the work schedule
   B. No, it doesn't.
   C. the salary

6. *A:* Do you have a full-time job?
   B: No, I don't. I only work 20 hours a week.

   Does the woman work full-time or part-time?
   A. full-time
   B. 20 hours a week
   C. part-time

Activity 2 (page 58)
1. *A:* Good morning. Bob's Auto Shop.
   B: I'm calling about the mechanic position. Do I need a driver's license for this job?
   A: **A.** Yes, you do.
   B. a driver's license
   C. ten o'clock

2. *A:* Central Movie Theater. How may I help you?
   B: Do I need computer skills for the cashier position?
   A: **A.** No, he doesn't.
   B. Yes, you do.
   C. a driver's license

3. *A:* Do you like your new job?
   B: Yes, I do. I like my job very much.
   A: **A.** That's too bad.
   B. That's good. I'm happy that you like your job.
   C. I don't have work experience.

4. *A:* I'm calling about the gardener position. Does the schedule include weekends?
   B: Yes, it does. The schedule includes Saturdays and Sundays.
   A: **A.** Thank you for the information.
   B. 12:30 [twelve thirty]
   C. No, it doesn't.

5. *A:* Do you earn a good salary?
   B: No, I don't. My pay is low.
   A: **A.** That's good.
   B. I'm sorry. That's too bad.
   C. $6.00 [six dollars] per hour.

6. *A:* Good morning. Bob's Family Restaurant.
   B: I'm calling about the cashier position. Do I need experience?
   A: **A.** Collect money and make change.
   B. $8.50 [eight fifty] per hour
   C. No you don't. You don't need experience for this job.

LESSON 6 Activity 3 (page 64)
Ad A
A: Good morning. Bob's Family Restaurant. How may I help you?
B: I'm calling about the assistant cook's position. Does the job include weekends?
A: Yes, it does. The work schedule is Tuesday through Sunday.
B: Thank you for the information.

Ad B

A: Hello. Gas Mart.
B: I'm calling about the cashier job. When does the job begin?
A: It begins next week.
B: Did you say next week?
A: Yes, next week.
B: Thank you very much.

Ad C

A: Florida Auto. Jan speaking.
B: This is David Brown. I have some questions about the auto salesperson position.
A: Okay. I can help you.
B: Does the work schedule include weekends?
A: Yes, it does. The salesperson works both Saturday and Sunday.
B: And when does the job begin?
A: The job begins immediately.
B: I have one more question. Is this a part-time, or full-time position?
A: It's full time.
B: Thank you very much!

UNIT 5

LESSON 2 Activity 4 (page 73)

1. Kim cut her knee and hurt her forehead.
2. Sandra broke her leg.
3. Minh hurt his elbow.
4. Martin sprained his wrist.
5. Tom sprained his ankle.
6. Victor hurt his back.

LESSON 3 Activity 1 (page 74)

1. A: City Medical Offices. This is Dr. Fong's nurse. How may I help you?
   B: I'd like to make an appointment with Dr. Fong.

   What does the man want?
   A. An appointment with Dr. Fong.
   B. An appointment with Dr. Fong's nurse.
   C. A job at the City Medical Offices.

2. A: What do you need to see the doctor about?
   B: I hurt my ankle.

   What is Martin's problem?
   A. He hurt his back.
   B. He hurt his knee.
   C. He hurt his ankle.

3. A: I need to see the doctor.
   B: What's the problem?
   A: I fell down and hurt my knee . It's really bad.

   What happened to Martin?
   A. He cut his knee.
   B. He fell down and hurt his knee.
   C. bandage Martin's knee.

4. A: The doctor can see you at 2:00 tomorrow.
   B: 2:00 tomorrow. That's fine. Thanks.

   When is Martin's appointment?
   A. tomorrow at 2:00 [two o'clock]
   B. tomorrow at 2:30 [two thirty]
   C. Tuesday at 2:00 [two o'clock]

Activity 3 (page 79)

A: Now I'd like to ask you about your family medical history.
B: Okay.
A: Do you have any history of heart disease in your family? Is there any family history of heart attacks?
B: Yes, my father had a heart attack last year.

A: Does anyone in your family have high blood pressure?
B: My father has high blood pressure. It started in….um… 2004. He takes medication for it.
A: Okay. Does anyone in your family have diabetes?
B: Yes, my mother has diabetes.
A: When did her diabetes start?
B: Oh, it started about….five years ago.
A: How about asthma? Is there any asthma in your family?
B: No, I don't think so.

LESSON 6 Activity 2 (page 80)

A: 911 Operator.
B: I have an emergency!
A: What's the problem?
B: My daughter swallowed kitchen cleanser. She's only four years old!
A: When did it happen?
B: It happened about five minutes ago.
A: Okay. Did you give her any water to drink?
B: No, I gave her a glass of milk.
A: Do not give her milk. Give her a large glass of water. What is your address?
B: It's 4232 Lincoln Street.
A: Okay. Don't hang up. An ambulance is coming.

UNIT 6

LESSON 2 Activity 3 (page 89)

1. Did the housekeeper make the bed? Yes, she did. She made the bed.
2. Did the painter paint the wall? No, he didn't. He painted the door.
3. Did the salesclerk sell a clock? Yes, she did. She sold a clock.
4. Did the stockperson stock the shelves? No, he didn't. He didn't stock the shelves yet.
5. Did the chef prepare the dinner? Yes, he did. He prepared a nice dinner.
6. Did the plumber fix the sink? Yes, she did.
7. Did the delivery person deliver the boxes? Yes, she did. She delivered two boxes.
8. Did the carpenter repair the door? No, he didn't. He repaired the wall.

LESSON 3 Activity 1 (page 90)

1. A: Did you repair Mr. Johnson's truck?
   B: No, I didn't. I repaired Mrs. Brown's car.

   What did the man do yesterday?
   A. He repaired Mr. Johnson's truck.
   B. No, he didn't.
   C. He repaired Mrs. Brown's car.

2. A: Did you deliver the packages to Mr. Jones?
   B: Yes, I did. I delivered them at 2:00.

   Did the man deliver the packages?
   A. 2:00
   B. Yes, he did.
   C. Mr. Jones.

3. A: That's five dollars and fifty cents.
   B: Here's a five-dollar bill and two quarters.
   A: Thank you very much. Have a nice day.

   Did the cashier give change?
   A. Yes, he did.
   B. No, he didn't.
   C. Five dollars and fifty cents.

4. A: Did you sell a jacket to the customer?
   B: No, I didn't. I sold a shirt.

What did the salesman do?
A. He sold a shirt
B. No, he didn't.
C. He sold a jacket.

Activity 2 (page 90)
A: Let's talk about your work today, Amina. Did you write the paychecks?
B: Yes, I did.
A: And did you make copies of the paychecks?
B: No, I didn't.
A: That's OK. You can make copies of the paychecks tomorrow. Did you check email?
B: Yes, I did. I checked the email this afternoon.
A: Did you call Mr. Jones?
B: Yes, I did. I called Mr. Jones this morning.
A: And did you send the package to Mrs. Green?
B: I'm sorry, but I didn't send the package. I didn't have time.
A: That's okay. You can send the package tomorrow. How about my letters? Did you deliver the letters to the post office?
B: Yes, I did. I delivered all the letters.
A: Thank you, Amina. You are an excellent office assistant!
B: Thank you, Mr. Brown. I like my job!

LESSON 5 Activity 3 (page 95)
A: What did you do at your last job, Jack?
B: I delivered refrigerators and ovens.
A: Did you repair the refrigerators and ovens?
B: No, I didn't.
A: Who did you report to?
B: I reported to the assistant manager.
A: Why did you leave that job?
B: I left because the business closed.
A: I see you have a college degree. When did you graduate?
B: I graduated two months ago.
A: Congratulations.
B: Thank you.

UNIT 7

LESSON 2 Activity 1 (page 104)
1. A: Was it sunny in Miami?
   B: Yes, it was.
2. A: Where was it foggy?
   B: It was foggy in San Francisco.
3. A: How was the weather in Chicago?
   B: It was cold.
4. A: Was it freezing in San Diego?
   B: No, it was raining.

Activity 4 (page 105)
Last month, Pat and Terry took their children on a trip. Pat was nervous. The weather was terrible and driving was dangerous. Terry was calm and happy. He likes to travel with his wife and children. For their son, Jamie, the trip was great. He was excited. He liked the car trip and he enjoyed listening to music. For their daughter, Logan, the trip was awful. She wasn't comfortable. She didn't like sitting next to the dog. She doesn't want to go on another trip in the car for a LONG time.

LESSON 3 Pronunciation Activity B (page 106)
1. Was he in class?
2. Was it early?
3. Was he worried?
4. Was she excited?
5. Was it in Dallas?
6. Who was he with?
7. Where was it?
8. Why was she nervous?

LESSON 3 Activity 1 (page 106)
A: How was your trip to Miami?
B: It was great!
A: Did you fly?
B: No, I didn't. I took a train. It was a long ride. But I was comfortable.
A: Well, welcome back to work.
B: Thanks. It was a nice trip, but I'm glad to be back.

Activity 2 (page 106)
1. A: How was your trip to Miami, Jose?
   B: It was great! Miami is a beautiful city.

   Where did the man go?
   A. San Diego.
   B. Miami.
   C. Los Angeles.

2. A: Did you fly?
   B: No, I didn't. I took a train. It was a long ride. But I was comfortable.

   How did the man travel?
   A. He traveled by train.
   B. Yes, he did.
   C. He traveled by car.

3. A: How was your trip?
   B: It was great, but I was tired.

   How was the man's trip?
   A. Terrible
   B. Yes, it was.
   C. Great.

4. A: How was the weather in Miami?
   B: It was hot and rainy. I was not comfortable.

   How was the weather in Miami?
   A. Cold and rainy
   B. Beautiful
   C. Hot and rainy

5. A: How was your trip to New York?
   B: It was awful. The weather was freezing. I was not comfortable.

   Where did the woman go?
   A. freezing
   B. Awful
   C. New York

6. A: How was your trip to New York?
   B: It was awful. The weather was freezing. I was not comfortable.

   How was the woman's trip?
   A. freezing
   B. awful
   C. New York

LESSON 5 Activity 1 (page 110)
100 years ago, New York City was a very different place than it is today. The average salary for workers was $300 a year. Today the average salary is $49,000 per year. The price of food was also much cheaper 100 years ago. In the early 1900s, beef cost 10 cents a pound. Now it costs about four dollars and forty-nine cents a pound. There are more people in New York City now . There were about 2 million people in the city 100 years ago. Now the population is 8.2 million!

LESSON 6 Activity 2 (page 112)
1. Reston is more modern than Mitchell.
2. Mitchell is more crowded than Reston.
3. Rents in Reston are lower than rents in Mitchell.

4. Minh's family liked Mitchell
5. The school in Reston is better than the school in Mitchell.
6. Minh and his family moved to Reston.

UNIT 8

LESSON 2 Activity 4 (page 121)
1. Pedro bought a lot of milk.
2. Pedro bought two cans of soup.
3. Pedro bought a couple of tomatoes.
4. Pedro bought a little bit of cereal.
5. Pedro bought one bunch of bananas.
6. Pedro bought some chicken.

LESSON 3 Activity 1 (page 122)
1. *A:* Where are the people?
   B: Good evening. Are you ready to order?
   A: Yes, I'm ready.

   Where are the people?
   A. In a kitchen.
   B. In a restaurant.
   C. At the man's house.

2. *A:* Good evening. Are you ready to order?
   B: Yes, I'm ready.
   A: OK. Would you like to start with soup or a salad? We have a great onion soup or a nice green salad.

   Who is the man?
   A. A customer.
   B. A server.
   C. A cook.

3. *A:* OK. Would you like to start with a soup or a salad? We have a great onion soup or a nice green salad.
   B: No, thank you. What kind of sandwiches do you have?
   A: We have chicken, tuna, and steak. We also have hamburgers and cheeseburgers.
   B: I'd like a chicken sandwich.
   A: All right. Would you like a soda with that?
   B: No, but I'll have an iced tea, please.

   What does the woman order for dinner?
   A. A chicken sandwich and an iced tea.
   B. A chicken salad and an iced tea.
   C. A chicken sandwich and a soda.

4. *A:* How was everything?
   B: It was great. Thank you.
   A: Would you like to order some dessert?
   B: Yes, I would like a piece of chocolate cake.
   A: OK.

   How was the woman's meal?
   A. It was great.
   B. It was awful.
   C. a piece of chocolate cake.

Unit 9

LESSON 3 Activity 1 (page 138)
1. *A:* Hello. I'm calling about the two-bedroom apartment on Lake Street. Does it have a washer and dryer?
   B: Yes, it does.

   What size apartment does the caller ask about?
   A. 1-bedroom.
   B. 2-bedroom.
   C. 3-bedroom.

2. *A:* Are pets allowed?
   B: Yes, they are.
   A: Does the apartment have a washer and dryer?
   B: Yes, it does. The washer and dryer are behind the kitchen.

   Are pets allowed?
   A. Yes, they are.
   B. No, they aren't.
   C. The caller doesn't ask about pets.

3. *A:* Hello. Pine Valley Apartments.
   B: How much is the rent for your apartments?
   A: The 1-bedroom apartment is $750. The 2-bedroom apartment is $850. And the three-bedroom apartment is $1000.
   B: Thank you for the information.

   How much is the rent for the 1-bedroom apartment?
   A. $850
   B. $750
   C. $1,000

4. *A:* Hello. I'm calling about the apartment on Elm Street. Is it furnished?
   B: No, it isn't. It's unfurnished.
   A: Thank you for the information.

   Does the apartment on Elm Street have furniture?
   A. No, it doesn't
   B. Yes, it does.
   C. It's on Elm Street.

5. *A:* Where do you shop for food?
   B: I shop at Bob's supermarket because it's the cheapest supermarket in the neighborhood.

   Why does the woman shop at Bob's Supermarket?
   A. It's close to her house.
   B. Bob's Supermarket
   C. It's the cheapest supermarket in the neighborhood.

6. *A:* What street do you live on? I live on Cherry Street.
   B: Oh that's very quiet. I live on Maple Street.
   A: Maple Street? Oh, that is the busiest street in the neighborhood!
   B: It's very noisy, too.

   What is the busiest street in the neighborhood?
   A. Cherry Street
   B. Maple Street
   C. quiet street

Pronunciation Activity B (page 143)
1. than
2. day
3. their
4. lather
5. den
6. those

LESSON 6 Activity 2 (page 144)
A: How can I help you today?
B: Hi. I'm looking for a new cell phone plan.
A: With our lowest rate, you get 3,000 minutes a month.
B: How much does that plan cost?
A: That plan is $29.95 [twenty-nine ninety five] a month.
B: That's great. Can I get a free phone if I sign up with your company?
A: Yes, you can. You can choose from three free phones.
B: Which phones are free?
A: These three phones are the free phones.
B: Thank you.

Activity 3 (page 144)
1. *A:* Can I help you?
   B: Yes. Can you tell me about your plans?

A: Sure. We offer a great plan for $39.95 a month.
B: How many minutes do you offer?
A: We offer 3,500 minutes for that price.
B: Do you offer a free cell phone?
A: No, we don't offer a free phone, but if you sign up today, you get a free wireless headset.
B: How much does a camera phone cost?
A: This phone has the lowest price. It's $85.00. This is our most expensive phone. It's $350.
B: I see. Thank you very much.
A: You're welcome.
2. A: How may I help you?
B: Hello, I'm looking for a new cell phone plan.
A: Well, we have a plan for $35.95 a month.
B: How many minutes does it include?
A: It includes 3,000 minutes.
B: Do you offer a free cell phone?
A: Yes, we do. You can choose from these two camera phones.
B: How much do these phones usually cost?
A: They cost $150 each.
B: OK. Thank you for your help.
A: You're welcome.
3. A: May I help you?
B: Yes, I'm shopping for a new cell phone plan. How much is your lowest rate?
A: Our lowest rate is $34.95 a month.
B: How many minutes are included?
A: That plan includes 2,000 minutes a month and free weekends.
B: Do you offer a free cell phone?
A: No, we don't. But we offer a free wireless headset if you sign up.
B: I like this black phone. How much does this phone cost?
A: This phone is $160.

Unit 10

LESSON 3 Activity 1 (page 154)

1. A: Your license is expired. You have to renew it immediately.
   B: OK, officer. I will go to the DMV right away.

   What does the man have to do?
   A. Renew his driver's license.
   B. Pay for a ticket
   C. Apply for a driver's license.

2. A: I want to renew my license. What do I have to do?
   B: You have to pay the fee. It's $30.

   What does the man have to do?
   A. Pay $13.
   B. Apply for a driver's license.
   C. Pay $30.

3. A: Do I have to take a written test?
   B: Yes, you do. But we're very busy today. You can take the test next week.

   Does the man have to take his test today?
   A. Yes, he does.
   B. No, he doesn't. He can take the test next week.
   C. A written test.

4. A: Did I pass the test?
   B: No, I'm sorry, you didn't. You have to take the driving test again.

   What does the man have to do?
   A. He has to take the written test again.
   B. He has to take the driving test again.
   C. No, he didn't.

LESSON 6 Activity 2 (page 160)

A: Hi, Carl. Sorry I'm late. I'm lost. Can you give me directions to Millie's Restaurant?
B: Sure, Gloria. Where are you now?
A: I'm walking past the school. The school is on my right.
B: OK. Walk to Cherry Street. Turn right on Cherry Street. Then walk down Cherry toward the bank. Go north on Pine Street and turn right on Peach Street. Turn left on Fir street. Millie's restaurant is in the middle of the block on Fir Street.
A: Thanks. I'll meet you at the restaurant in about 10 minutes.

Unit 11

LESSON 3 Pronunciation Activity B (page 170)

1. We're going to go to a movie.
2. I'm shopping.
3. Are you going to stay home?
4. I'm going to have Marta over for dinner.
5. He's taking it easy.
6. We're going to go shopping on Sunday.

Activity 1 (page 170)

1. A: What are you going to do this weekend, Jill?
   B: My parents are going to visit me. I'm going to do a lot of things with them on Saturday and Sunday.

   What are Ed and Jill talking about?
   A. vacation plans
   B. weekend plans
   C. Friday night plans

2. A: Where are you and your parents going to go this weekend, Jill?
   B: We're going to go to the beach on Saturday. On Sunday, we're going to go shopping and then we're going to see a movie.

   What are Jill and her parents going to do on Saturday?
   A. They're going to see a movie.
   B. They're going to go to the beach.
   C. They're going to go shopping.

3. A: How about you, Ed? What are you going to do this weekend?
   B: I'm going to see a movie on Saturday night. And I'm going to invite some friends for dinner on Sunday.
   A: Oh, that sounds like a nice weekend.

   What is Ed going to do on Sunday?
   A. He's going to invite some friends for dinner.
   B. He's going to see a movie.
   C. No, he isn't.

4. A: What are your plans for the weekend, David?
   B: My wife and I are going to go shopping on Saturday morning. Then my son and I are going to go to a soccer game on Saturday afternoon. My son loves soccer. On Sunday, I'm just going to relax and take it easy!

   What is David going to do on Sunday?
   A. He's going to go to a soccer game.
   B. He and his wife are going to go shopping.
   C. He's going to relax.

LESSON 5 Activity 1 (page 174)

1. get dressed up
2. give someone a gift
3. watch fireworks
4. have a picnic

Activity 4 (page 175)

A: What are you going to do for President's Day weekend, Sue?
B: I'm going to go to Miami to visit my family. My sister's birthday is on Saturday.
A: Are you going to have a party for her?

B: Yes, we are. I'm going to make a cake. I might cook dinner, too. How about you, Alan? Are you going to go anywhere?
A: I'm going to go to San Francisco.
B: What are you going to do there?
A: I'm going to go hiking with my brother. I might visit some old friends, too.

LESSON 6 Activity 1 (page 176)
1. Lucy is going to go to English class on Monday, Wednesday, and Friday.
2. Lucy might get a haircut on Tuesday.
3. She might see a movie on Tuesday night.
4. On Wednesday, she might go hiking.
5. She might have lunch with Alan on Thursday.
6. She is going to go to a party on Friday night.
7. On Saturday, she is going to go to the beach.
8. She might work on a project on Sunday.

Unit 12

LESSON 2 Activity 1 (page 184)
1. Linh wants to be a pharmacist.
2. Ivan wants to get a job.
3. Joseph and Sara want to purchase a home.
4. Luisa wants to graduate from college
5. Teresa and Marcus want to send their children to college.

LESSON 3 Activity 1 (page 186)
1. I want to be an auto mechanic. First, I need to go to a job training class for mechanics. I will be a good mechanic.
2. My goal is to go to college. First, I need to learn more English. Then I plan to apply to college. English is difficult!
3. I want to be a citizen. First, I have to fill out the papers for the naturalization application. It's a lot of work to fill out all the papers.
4. My wife and I want to purchase a home. First we need to save a lot of money. Houses are expensive!

Activity 2 (page 186)
1. *A:* Ivan, What is your goal?
   B: I want to be a mechanic.
   A: What is your first step?
   B: I need to go to job training classes for mechanics.

   What is Ivan's goal?
   A. be a police officer
   B. be a teacher
   C. be a mechanic

2. *A:* Is your son going to graduate from college this year?
   B: Yes, he is. I'm very proud of him.
   A: What does he plan to do?
   B: He plans to open his own business.

   What does the son plan to do after college?
   A. Yes, he does.
   B. He plans to open his own business.
   C. He wants to graduate from college.

3. *A:* See you later – I'm going to the police station.
   B: Why are you going there?
   A: I need to get a background check . Then I can become a U.S. citizen.

   Where is the man going?
   A. to the U.S.
   B. to the police station
   C. to Ghana

4. *A:* What is your goal?
   B: Well, my wife and I have 5 children. We need a bigger house. We want to buy a house in the next 3 or 4 years.

   How many children does the man have?
   A. three
   B. four
   C. five

Activity 3 (page 186)
1. *A:* Students, do you have any questions about citizenship?
   B: Do I need to take a citizenship test to become a U.S. citizen?
   A: **A.** Yes, you do.
   B. at the state building.
   C. in July.

2. *A:* Oh, look! My new U.S. passport just arrived in the mail!
   B: That's great! Where do you plan to travel?
   A: **A.** Yes, I do.
   B. U.S. passport
   C. to Mexico.

3. *A:* Bob, what do you plan to do after you graduate?
   B: Well, I'm going to get married next summer, and after that, I plan to find a job.
   A: **A.** I'm sorry to hear that.
   B. You're getting married? Congratulations!
   C. Next week.

4. *A:* City of Jamestown. Can I help you?
   B: Yes, I want to vote in the election next week. Where do I go to vote?
   A: **A.** It's on Tuesday.
   B. Voting will be at the library on Oak St.
   C. Thank you.

5. *A:* What are you going to do during vacation?
   B: I plan to volunteer at the Senior Center.
   A: **A.** I don't know.
   B. Volunteer? That's a nice thing to do.
   C. I'm sorry, I don't.

6. *A:* Springfield Adult Learning. Can I help you?
   B: Yes, I want to take a citizenship class. When does your next class start?
   A: **A.** Yes, we do.
   B. What's your name?
   C. It starts on April 3.

LESSON 5 Pronunciation Activity C (page 190)
1. This year he won't travel to his hometown.
2. They'll be getting married in July.
3. She'll vote in the election next November.
4. I won't start work until 7:30.
5. He won't apply for a student loan next year.
6. I'll study hard so I can graduate this year.
7. They won't be taking ESL classes in the spring.
8. Next February, you'll complete your ESL course.

Vocabulary

Numbers in parentheses indicate unit numbers.

a couple of (8)
a few (8)
a little bit of (8)
a lot of (8)
account (2)
across (10)
adult (1)
afraid (7)
afternoon (3)
ago (5)
allergy (5)
allow (9)
always (3)
ankle (5)
anniversary (11)
antibiotic (5)
antihistamine (5)
application (4)
apply (2)
appointment (2)
arm (5)
around (10)
assist (4)
assistant (4)
bus driver (4)
ATM machine (2)
attend (3)
auto mechanic (12)
average (7)
away from (10)
awful (7)
back (5)
background check (12)
bag (8)
banana (8)
bandage (5)
bank (10)
bathroom (9)
beach (11)
bean (8)
beard (1)
beautiful (7)
become (12)
bedroom (9)
benefit (4)
best (9)
better (7)
bill (6)
birthday (11)
block (9)
blonde (1)
blood pressure (5)
blueberry (8)
bookcase (6)
bottle (8)
box (8)
bread (8)
break (4)
broccoli (8)
brother-in-law (1)
build (6)
building (7)

bunch (8)
burn (5)
bus (7)
busy (7)
cable company (9)
calcium (8)
calf (5)
calm (7)
calorie (8)
can (8)
car (7)
carpenter (6)
carpet (3)
carrot (8)
carton (8)
cash (2)
cashier (4)
cast (5)
catch (5)
celebrate (11)
cereal (8)
change (2)
cheap (9)
check (6)
check email (3)
check out (2)
cheek (5)
chef (4)
chest (5)
chicken (8)
child care worker (12)
chin (5)
chips (8)
choke (5)
chore (3)
citizen (12)
citizenship (12)
clean (7)
close (9)
closet (9)
coffee (8)
cold (7)
collect (4)
college (1)
comfortable (7)
complete (12)
computer technician (6)
convenience store (9)
conversation (3)
cook (4)
cough syrup (5)
coupon (2)
cousin (1)
cracker (8)
cream (5)
credit card (2)
crosswalk (10)
cry (5)
curly (1)
custodian (1)
cut (5)
dairy (8)

dance (11)
dangerous (9)
daughter-in-law (1)
day/night shift (4)
deadline (12)
degree (4)
deliver (6)
delivery person (6)
dentist (5)
department (2)
department store (9)
deposit (2)
design (6)
dining room (9)
divorced (1)
DMV (10)
do (3)
door (6)
down (10)
drive (10)
driver's license (10)
driving test (10)
drug store (9)
dryer (9)
ear (5)
earn (4)
east (10)
egg (8)
elbow (5)
Election Day (11)
election (12)
electric company (9)
electrician (9)
elementary school (1)
emergency (5)
emergency room (5)
employee (4)
energetic (5)
engaged (1)
engine (6)
every (3)
every day (3)
excited (7)
exciting (7)
exercise (5)
expensive (7)
experience (4)
expire (10)
expired (2)
exterminator (9)
eye (5)
eye exam (3)
fall (5)
Father's Day (11)
fee (2)
feel (5)
fill out (2)
financial aid (12)
find out (6)
finger (5)
fire station (10)

fireworks (11)
flight attendant (4)
flight (7)
fly (4)
foggy (7)
follow-up (5)
forehead (5)
freckles (1)
freezing (7)
friendly (7)
fruits (8)
full-time (4)
furnished (9)
furniture store (9)
garage (9)
gardener (4)
garlic (8)
gas company (9)
get (5)
get married (11)
get ready (3)
give (5)
glasses (1)
go (5)
go out (11)
goal (12)
grade (1)
graduate (12)
graduation (11)
grains (8)
granddaughter (1)
grandfather (1)
grandparent (1)
grandson (1)
grapes (8)
great (7)
gym (3)
haircut (3)
hand (5)
happy (7)
hardware store (9)
hardwood floor (9)
have (5)
have to (10)
health insurance (4)
heart attack (5)
heel (5)
help (3)
high school (1)
high school diploma (4)
high (7)
hike (11)
hip (5)
hit (5)
hometown (7)
housekeeper (6)
housework (3)
how many (3)
how often (3)
hurt (5)
include (4)
Independence Day (11)

inhaler (5)
inspect (4)
install (6)
intersection (10)
interview (12)
into (10)
invite (11)
iron (8)
jam (8)
jar (8)
job (12)
join (5)
juice (8)
ketchup (8)
kindergarten (1)
knee (5)
large (7)
late fee (2)
laundry (3)
lazy (7)
learner's permit (10)
leave (6)
lemon (8)
librarian (12)
library card (2)
library (10)
license (4)
lip (5)
living room (9)
load (6)
loaf (8)
loan (12)
locksmith (9)
lose (5)
lounge (4)
low (7)
mail (2)
make (5)
manager (4)
marry (12)
may (2)
mechanic (6)
middle school (1)
might (11)
milk (8)
modern (7)
morning (3)
mother (1)
Mother's Day (11)
mother-in-law (1)
mover (6)
movie theater (10)
museum (10)
music (3)
mustache (1)
mustard (8)
nap (3)
naturalization application (12)
need (4)
neighborhood (7)
nervous (7)
never (3)
new (7)
noisy (7)
north (10)

nose (5)
nurse (3)
Oath of Allegiance (12)
offer (4)
office assistant (6)
oil (8)
old (7)
olive oil (8)
onion (8)
out of (10)
over (10)
overdue (2)
overtime (4)
pack (6)
package (2)
pain reliever (5)
painter (6)
part time (3)
pass (10)
passport (12)
past (10)
pasta (8)
patient (4)
pay (6)
pay back (12)
peanut butter (8)
pedestrian (10)
pepper (8)
pet (9)
pharmacist (12)
pharmacy (9)
phone company (9)
pick up (2)
picnic (11)
pilot (4)
plan (4)
plane (7)
plastic (2)
plumber (6)
population (7)
post-secondary (1)
pound (5)
practice (10)
pregnant (1)
preschool (1)
prescription (5)
President's Day (11)
price (2)
principal (1)
probably (11)
process (12)
project (11)
protein (8)
proud (12)
purchase (12)
put (5)
quiet (7)
rainy (7)
rarely (3)
reach (12)
receipt (2)
reference (6)
refund (2)
relax (11)
relaxed (7)

renew (10)
rent (7)
repair (3)
repair person (6)
report (to) (6)
require (4)
requirement (12)
research (12)
restroom
return (2)
rice (8)
run (11)
safe (9)
salary (4)
sales tax (2)
salesperson (4)
salt (8)
save (12)
schedule (4)
scholarship (12)
school counselor (1)
school (10)
security guard/agent (4)
see (5)
sell (6)
semester (12)
send (12)
server (6)
serving (8)
set (3)
several (8)
shin (5)
shoe store (10)
shop (11)
shoulder (5)
sister (1)
skill (4)
small (7)
snack (3)
sodium (8)
some (8)
sometimes (3)
son (1)
soup (8)
south (10)
speed limit (10)
spinach (8)
sprain (5)
stay home (11)
stay up (11)
steak (8)
stitch (5)
stockperson (6)
stomach (5)
stop sign (10)
store credit (2)
straight (1)
street (7)
stressful (7)
strong (5)
success (12)
sunny (7)
superintendent (9)
supermarket (9)
supervise (4)

sure (11)
swallow (5)
take (3)
take it easy (11)
tall (7)
tea (8)
teacher's aide (4)
test (12)
text message (3)
thigh (5)
throat (5)
through (10)
thumb (5)
ticket (10)
toe (5)
toward (10)
traditional (7)
traffic light (10)
train (4)
trip (7)
tuition (12)
tuna (8)
turn (10)
turning lane (10)
twins (1)
uncomfortable (7)
under (10)
unfurnished (9)
union (4)
up (10)
usually (3)
vacation day (4)
vacuum (6)
vegetable (8)
visit (5)
volunteer (12)
vote (12)
want (12)
washer (9)
wavy (1)
wedding (11)
weekend (11)
west (10)
widowed (1)
windy (7)
winter vacation (1)
withdraw (2)
working conditions (4)
worried (7)
worse (7)
wrap (5)
wrist (5)
written test (10)
yesterday (5)
yield (10)
yogurt (8)

Index

Academic Skills

Credits

Illustrators: Fian Arroyo, Richard Beacham, Steve Bjorkman, David Cole, Julia Durgee, Stephen Elford, Noel Ford, Kent Gamble, Janise Gates, Jerry Gonzalez, Terry Guyer, Jim Haynes, David Hillman, Michael Hortens, Garrett Kallenbach, Kevin Kobasic, Karen Lee, Tania Lee, Shelton Leong, Pat Lewis, Erin Mauterer, Scott McBee, Joe Nendza, Eric Olson, Geo Parkin, Rich Powell, Zak Pullen, Bot Roda, Jon Rogers, Scott Ross, Daniel Rubinstein, Ray Russotto, Theresa Seeyle, Peter Smith, Jem Sullivan, Stephen Sweny, Alan Wade, Ron Zalme, Jerry Zimmerman

Photo credits:

2 Jack Hollingsworth / Getty Images, 5 Photodisc / SuperStock, 11 Digital Vision / Alamy, Jon Feingersh / Masterfile, Hans Bjurling / Getty Images, Redchopsticks.com LLC / Alamy, Richard Church / Alamy, JUPITERIMAGES/ Brand X / Alamy 17 Digital Vision / Getty Images, Redchopsticks. com / SuperStock, Blend Images / SuperStock, Radius Images / Alamy, David Young-Wolff / Alamy, 19 Margot Granitsas / The Image Works, 26 Jeff Greenberg / The Image Works, 27 Purestock / Alamy, Blend Images / SuperStock, Blend Images / SuperStock, Photodisc / SuperStock, Peter Hvizdak / The Image Works, Masterfile Royalty Free (RF), 31 Bruce Laurance / Getty Images, 34 JUPITERIMAGES/ Comstock Images / Alamy, 35 JUPITERIMAGES/ Thinkstock / Alamy, 41 Image Source / SuperStock, 43 China Tourism Press / Getty Images, Chris Ware / The Image Works, AP Photo/St. Cloud Times, Jason Wachter, Andersen Ross / Getty Images, JUPITERIMAGES/ Polka Dot / Alamy, David R. Frazier / The Image Works, 49 Comstock Select / Corbis, Vario images GmbH & Co.KG / Alamy, Blend Images / Alamy 50 Ariel Skelley/CORBIS, Image Source / SuperStock , 59 Masterfile Royalty Free (RF), Photofusion Picture Library / Alamy, Bob Daemmrich / The Image Works, Blend Images / Alamy, Martin Rose/ Bongarts / Getty Images, moodboard / Alamy 65 Blend Images / Getty Images, Bambu Productions / Getty Images, Adam Burn, Comstock / SuperStock, Bob Daemmrich / The Image Works, Stewart Cohen / Getty Images, 75 The Image Works, 82 Jack Hollingsworth / Getty Images, 91 Andersen Ross / Getty Images, Photodisc / SuperStock, SW Productions/Brand X/Corbis, Deepak Buddhiraja/India Picture/Corbis 97 Kate Mitchell/zefa/Corbis 98 Jack Hollingsworth/Corbis , Andy Nelson / The Christian Science Monitor / Getty Images, VEER Brian Donnelly / Getty Images 107 Ray Laskowitz / SuperStock, Blend Images / SuperStock, Rayes / Digital Vision / Agpix, Corbis, Digital Vision / Alamy, Bubbles Photolibrary / Alamy, 110 Bettmann/CORBIS, 123 JUPITERIMAGES/ Creatas / Alamy, 129 LWA-Dannm Tardif / CORBIS, 130 Foodcollection.com / Alamy, 131 Photodisc / SuperStock, 138 Jeff Greenberg/ The Image Works, 139 Jose Luis Pelaez, Inc / CORBIS, 142 SW Productions / Brand X / Corbis, AP Photo/Journal Times, Mark Hertzberg, Kyoko Hamada / Getty Images, Design Pics/Corbis, Lee F. Snyder / Photo Researchers, Inc, Andreanna Seymore / Getty Images, Bill Lai / The Image Works, 144 Justin Sullivan / Bloomberg News / Landov, 145 Purestock / SuperStock, vPixtal / SuperStock, 146 Brand X / SuperStock, age fotostock / SuperStock, Digital Vision Ltd. / SuperStock, 147 age fotostock / SuperStock, age fotostock/ SuperStock 171 Ronnie Kaufman / Getty Images, 155 Syracuse Newspapers / Al Campanie / The Image Works, 161 Richard Lord / The Image Works 176 A. Huber/ U. Starke/ zefa/ Corbis, 177 Photodisc / SuperStock, 178 Tobi Zausner, Dennis Galante/ CORBIS, Somos Images LLC / Alamy, Blend Images / Alamy, 193 Spmda Dawes / The Image Works, 194 Corbis 195 Anton Vengo / SuperStock, Bob Daemmrich / The Image Works, Digital Vision Ltd. / SuperStock, Blend Images / SuperStock

Cover photo:

Hand: Getty
Dentist: Corbis
Smiling family: Corbis
Business woman: Corbis
Graduate: MMH